INTERPRETING AN AUTHOR'S WORDS

Refine Study and Writing Skills
By Understanding the Written Word

HOLLIS L. GREEN, ThD, PhD

INTERPRETING AN AUTHOR'S WORDS
Refine Study and Writing Skills By Understanding the Written Word
Copyright © 2008 by Hollis L. Green

Library of Congress Control Number: 2008906341

  Green, Hollis L. 1933 –
    Interpreting An Author's Words
    ISBN 978-0-9801674-7-4
    Subject Codes and Description: 1: LAN005560: Language and
    Discipline - Composition/Creative Writing   2: LAN005510:
    Language and Discipline -Composition   3: LIT00000:
    Literature - English - General

Printed in the United States of America

Published by
GlobalEdAdvancePress
37321-7635 USA
http://www.GlobalEdAdvance.org

**Dedicated to my friend and colleague
William G. Justice, Jr., DMin, DPhil, DLitt,
who faithfully continues to fulfill the
Scholar's Pledge**

PLEDGE TO SCHOLARSHIP

"I do solemnly commit myself, from this time forth, to serve God and my fellow beings by engaging in academic and professional pursuits that I believe beneficial to the family, the community, and the Church. I further resolve to commit unto others by written and spoken word that beneficial truth and that experience which faithful servants have committed unto me. This I do promise."

Table of Contents

INTRODUCTION

Types of Inquiry

Despite all of modern science's perceived wizardry and high-powered technology, human beings can inquire in only two basic ways, analysis, and synthesis. In analysis, one separates a perceived whole into its parts; in synthesis, one combines perceived parts into wholes. By these two actions, humans investigate existence. All observation is built on these two types of inquiry. Likewise, thought systems are dichotomous, being fundamentally inductive or deductive. Inquiry systems and thought systems are not unrelated. Inquiry can be made in both scientific and nonscientific disciplines through analysis and synthesis using deductive and inductive logic.

Two methods of correct thinking (reasoning) derive from this basic dichotomy of human inquiry --deduction and induction. Deductive logic moves from the perceived whole (the general case) to a part (the specific case). Inductive logic moves from the perceived parts (specific cases) to the whole (the general case). When inductive or deductive logic chains are performed unconsciously in the human brain, the resulting transformation is termed a hunch or an intuition.

Both synthesis and analysis, with their corresponding logic's induction and deduction, are used generally. Science involves human experience and knowledge remembers or stores experience. Consequently, the controlled experiment is a means of formally, rigorously, and objectively experiencing and recording a well defined human event.

This deductive process involving analysis is what commonly comes to mind when one thinks of scientific process. While few would deny that scientific analysis has made possible the technological breakthroughs of the modern age, many neglect the contribution of synthesis and the process of induction to these rapid and far-reaching advances. Synthesis is generally the process of establishing the assumptions from which interpretations are deduced. Interpretations deduced from false assumptions about the human experience cannot be empirically supported.

Academic-level reading is sophisticated research. It is a search for something in particular rather than reading for general information. Developmental readings are much the same as looking for a word in a dictionary or looking up a subject in an encyclopedia. One does not read the entire work. The effort is to search for something in particular. When the rules are followed it is not a difficult process. For example, looking for material on Zoology in an encyclopedia, one does not begin reading in the "A" section. The process of selecting information for a written document is simplified with logic and common sense.

The etymological meaning of the word research is "seek again." Today this word is commonly used to describe a wide range of activities concerned with human inquiry. Literally, the derived meaning suggests two fundamental characteristics, (1) diligence of inquiry and (2) a temporal relationship only to the present and past, although a basic purpose may be to extract a meaning that can be applied to the future.

Perhaps it is this latter characteristic that fixed the earliest inquiries on questions of origin and existence. A diligent searching again of the past reveals that existence, moving over time, has order, patterns, and sequences. The discovery of relationships that persisted over time made it possible to seek answers to questions about the future. Predictive instruments, such as calendars, were based on observed recurring patterns of the past. In reading, one learns through the same process.

As humans wrote down their observations, the effort to understand what was written began. To understand and interpret different aspects of human existence, various groups of scholars began to devise different schemes, but all used the basic method of inquiry. Eventually, sets of such methods were accepted as reliable by consensus of particular groups. Different groups were concerned with different aspects of human inquiry; and, consequently, the methodologies that evolved differed from group to group.

In its early history, research served at least a two-fold purpose: it sharpened the intellectual concerns of humans, and it assisted in developing theories to explain the universe. Human enlightenment was its goal. The earliest questions related to the universe, the grand scheme, not to such parts as the economic, social, cultural, political and anthropological aspects of human existence. Gradually, scientific prediction methods were adapted to more and more specific questions. As adaptation proliferated, disciplines emerged within the general process of scientific research.

Early in its development, the lack of systematic and objective observation restricted the progress of research. Thinking itself was not necessarily systematic. Overcoming this restriction required developing a way to systematically think about thinking. Thus, logic emerged.

Attributed to the Greeks, the early development of logic took the form of deductive reasoning. This system of logic derives conclusions from generalizations, that is, universally accepted assumptions. The idea that "the whole" influences "the part" is a principle of deductive thought. The philosophy of Socrates and Plato gave direction to the developments of thought and produced early concepts of social relationships among humans.

Aristotle continued this reshaping of human imagination by analyzing ideas based on generalizations that were inductively obtained. He observed commonalties among many objects and processes and concluded that these common traits probably existed for all such objects and processes. His relentless quest for new assertions and "facts" based on field observations added the dimension of empiricism to scientific research. When such concepts conflicted with pristine religious authority, they were often rejected by the community. Curiosity persisted; however, and people with academic orientation began to rely on "facts" that could be empirically confirmed. Notwithstanding the progress in human inquiry, the fall of Greek and Roman civilization caused dogma to be re-emphasized and empirical investigations to be largely neglected.

The Renaissance Period revived the thought process that encouraged a search for new knowledge. Major discoveries, such as new continents, expanded thinking about physics, economics, society, and human behavior generally. The age of Galileo and Newton strengthened the intellectual process of scientific inquiry. Numerous thinkers followed (e. g., Sir Thomas More, Machiavelli, Bacon, Hobbes, and Locke), each offering various insights into the nature and the function of the human experience. All, in one manner or another, sought to distinguish reality from fiction and superstition. Gradually, the reality that concerned scientific investigation came to be viewed in terms of physical attributes that could be empirically confirmed.

The Industrial Revolution witnessed a great emergence of intellectuals who continued inquiry into diverse social phenomena and added technological inventions. These thinkers developed increasingly more rigorous methods of research. As a consequence, philosophical and mathematical advances produced a dramatic increase in the number and variety of scientific discoveries. These could not be ignored and had major impact on human thought.

So rooted in the earliest awareness of a need for knowledge and the continuing search by generations of thinkers, the systematic process of investigation emerged, in spite of the hurdles of vested interests and lack of support from the general populous. The present concept of scientific methodology began to form during medieval times and developed into a full body of concepts and constructs in the modern age.

A basic problem in understanding an author's words relates to the language and culture. When words or thoughts are translated from one language and a particular culture to another, the meaning changes. These changes often go unnoticed and individuals apply a current definition to the words. In fact the meaning of words is in people. Words in English may not mean the same as when they were written. A few examples from Holy Scripture may validate this point.

A classic misunderstanding of the Great Commission has produced a self-defeating theology of coercion in an effort to compel people to "go and do" when the intent of the commission was clearly "as you go make disciples." An aorist participle was translated as an imperative that made an indirect command "As you go make disciples" into a direct command "Go!" The intent of the participle was personal action as individuals traveled about their daily lives. The present life-style evangelism is the closest to a clear understanding of what Christ meant in the commission. The Christian way was to be a life-style and the making of disciples an automatic part of the process. (Matthew 28:19, 20)

Another translation difficulty is found in Titus 2:14, the translation of "peculiar." In 1611 the word had the meaning of private property or that which belongs to a person to the exclusion of others. The KJV translators took the Latin *peculium* from Roman law meaning the property which a son, wife, or slave might hold as his own, or to be over and above. This was clearly understood in medieval England because the King and Lords had total claim on their subjects. Although it may be good theology: that Jesus died to make believers His personal possession, the word "peculiar" was misunderstood by the early Holiness Movement in the US which established a peculiar dress and life-style to be different from the rest of the world. One can easily see how the word "peculiar" meant one thing in early England and another in parts of America.

Another word that creates problems in contemporary America is the word "blessed." In the Old Testament days and in early England the word "bless" meant "blood or blood-related." The legal construct of inheritance was established so property could be passed to blood relatives. Also, in the Old Testament the first born received a double portion of the inheritance because of birth order and blood-related priority.

This book has two objectives: to assist the reader in interpreting an author's words, and improving writing skills to make their own words better understood.

Topics Discussed in Chapter One

The Science of Interpretation
Classical Hermeneutics
Middle Ages and the Reformation
Religious Hermeneutics
Philosophical Hermeneutics
Literary Hermeneutics
Empirical Hermeneutics

HERMENEUTICS DEFINED

The Science of Interpretation

Hermeneutics is a word coined in the 17th century on the basis of the Greek *Hermeneuein,* "to interpret," which signified either a declamation of a text, an explanation of a situation or a translation from another language. *Hermeneuein* comes from the name of Hermes, the winged messenger god of ancient Greece, who delivered and explained the messages of the other gods.

As the science of interpretation, hermeneutics most often refers to interpretation of a written passage. In contemporary usage, it may refer to in-depth analysis of any written information and in research it includes analysis of statistical data. There are five types of hermeneutics: classical, religious, philosophical, literary, and empirical.

Classical Hermeneutics

The Ancient Greeks studied literature and regarded a written text as coherent whole rather than disjointed parts. They expected a text to have internal consistency in grammar, style, and ideas. The Greeks codified rules of grammar and style and used these rules to authenticate texts of uncertain origin.

Jewish Rabbis and the early Church Fathers used similar philological tools and became known for their allegorical interpretations. They found a hidden sense that agreed with their preconceived notions of what the literal text meant and used this same method in commentaries of the Vedas, Homer, the Koran and other sacred writings.

Middle Ages and the Reformation

Non-literal interpretations abounded during this period. Old Testament passages could be precursors of analogous material. New Testament episodes were considered to be symbolic lessons about the church or allegories of spiritual traits. Methodology began with imputing meaning into the text and then "finding" in the text a religious teaching consistent with tradition. The text was not allowed to speak for itself, because it was too obscure to read without church guidance

After Luther's translation of the Bible in to common German, Reformers insisted that Christians could rediscover their faith by reading the Bible themselves. Reformers viewed the text as responses to historical or social situations and the text could be clarified by studying contemporaneous Christian practice.

Religious Hermeneutics

Interpreting grammatically presupposed that words and expressions carry a relatively stable content during an era of history. It began with understanding the language in the plain sense and allowed for figures of speech, and determined that symbols, types, and/or special literary genre should be indicated by the text.

Interpreting historically considered the writer's and the

recipient's historical background and recovered the meaning of the words from another culture and another era. The process depended on what it meant to them in their culture and milieu: only trans-cultural principles can tell us what it means to us.

Interpreting critically was considered the only way to make rational sense out of a written text. The alternative was that one could make the text say whatever one wanted it to say. Written material was interpreted in the light of the context of the passage, progressive revelation, or interpreted scripture in harmony with other scripture. The unclear was interpreted in the light of the clear, the "spirit" of the passage in light of the literary genre, or with dependence upon the Holy Spirit.

Philosophical Hermeneutics

Friedrich Schleiermacher (1768-1834), a German theologian and philosopher, created a general hermeneutics based on classical methodology's focus on grammar and religious hermeneutics concern for themes. He approached a text with an effort to understand as if in a dialog with the text claiming that speaker and listener share language and that the listener understood words and sentences (grammar), and recognized intentions (common human nature). Schleiemacher's work involved projective introspection as well as intuitive linguistic analysis and had a grammatical thrust and a psychological thrust.

Schleiermacher's projective introspection was followed by Wilhelm Dilthey (1833-1911), a German philosopher, who made important contributions to a methodology for the humanities, objected to the pervasive influence of the natural sciences and developed a philosophy of life that perceived man in an historical contingency and changeability. Dilthey developed a hermeneutics for history and the human sciences that could produce objective knowledge. His methods utilized texts, verbal utterances, art, and actions are expressions whose "mental contents" (intentions) need comprehending and compared hermeneutic to interpreting a poem rather than doing physics or chemistry experiments.

Dilthey labeled this comprehension "understanding" as distinguished from explanatory knowledge of the hypothetico-deductive method. Dilthey, advanced that historians could relive and understand, but was criticized for reliance on introspection.   He revised his position to emphasize texts as products of their times.   Meanings were delineated by the author's worldview.   Dilthey designed a methodology for tracing a circle from author's biography and circumstances to the text to observe the affect.

Profoundly affected by the philosophy of Martin Heidegger, Hans-Georg Gadamer became the decisive figure in the development of hermeneutics, developing a distinctive and thoroughly dialogical approach. He critiqued the objectivity of hermeneutics because of reliance on the characterization of events and situations and developed an ontological hermeneutics that concentrated on the individual's apperception of experience from the inside out.

Jürgen Habermas, German philosopher and sociologist, developed a critical hermeneutic of universal pragmatics and argued that pragmatics should be studied in order to understand written material. He taught that understanding occurs in reference to a social situation and a historical setting in a dialogical way and believed that truth and meaning are negotiated by actors who come to consensus through social discourse. He also believed that understanding of language must be grounded in the practical purpose for which speakers use the language. Habermas taught that universal pragmatics was supposed to identify and reconstruct the preconditions for the possibility of understanding and concluded that the resulting critical hermeneutics made communication possible as participants overcame systematically distorted communication as they approach an ideal speech situation.

Literary Hermeneutics

According to Hirsch, validity in interpretation was the author's intent and the traditional definition of meaning. He excluded the author's mental processes at the time of writing would make objective meaning impossible because one cannot get inside the writer's head. This limited meaning to what is represented by the text as a whole and differentiated between intention and plan. Many acts are intended while few are planned and plans do not necessarily dictate what is written. Hirsch designated the interpreter, as author of text, is freed from the author and distinguished between meaning and significance. Meaning is what the text on the page represents and significance is the relationship of meaning and almost anything else.

The New Hermeneutics defined meaning as no longer something objective to be determined and described meaning as a subjective element arrived at through a circular experience the interpreter had with the text. The new process determined that any text written in another time period and culture contains a certain meaning for only that time period and culture and may have a totally different meaning for another time and culture or no meaning at all.

Empirical Hermeneutics

Empirical interpretation is closer to religious hermeneutics than philosophical and is the analysis of literature and previous studies related to a special topic. If the writing is recent and from our culture (or the culture being studied) there was no need to recover meanings of words or types of grammar. Words and expression carry a stable content.

The process required a special set of interpretation skills where the source can indicate bias. Evidence begs the question of how data were collected and/or presented. Omissions of details cause skepticism and logical filters need be applied to conclusions.

Regardless of the system of hermeneutics used to understand an author's words, one thing is clear: when words are translated from one language or culture to another, the meaning changes. It is this fact that requires a serious look at the author of a text, the time period of production, the author's intended audience, and how the meaning of words and technical terms have changed over time. If this is not done adequately the understanding of the author's words will be flawed and inconsistent when one attempts to make a contemporary application.

Understanding Hermeneutics Assists Reading

The better one understands the five types of hermeneutics and determines the particular process to be used in understanding developmental readings, the easier it is to turn reading into learning. During the process of reading, most individuals need guidance in interpreting what is read; therefore, a clear understanding of hermeneutics can make the process work.

Reading is not an end in itself; it is a process of covering new ground and learning new things. To fully comprehend and make use of what is read, a clear plan is needed.. Hermeneutics provides the framework for utilizing additive and variant findings in a constructive manner in a new composition

Topics Discussed in Chapter Two

Reading as an Art
Emphasis on Learning
Learning Logs
Learning Journal
Program Learning Chronicle

READING AND HERMENEUTICS

Reading as an Art

Art is the disposition or modification of things by human skill. Reading is an art. As such one can learn how to read and learn how to read better; consequently, most students need assistance with reading and interpreting what is read. The concept of reading for a degree in Europe was rejected in early American education because there were no libraries. The teacher was the only repository of knowledge and was the basis for the transferring knowledge to students. As libraries were constructed and books placed on the shelves, the teachers gave assignments to do collateral reading, but continued to lecture. The constant lecturing and the many reading assignments extended the required time to earn a degree. The reading was considered supplemental to the lecture, where in Europe it was instead of the lecture. Over time this process has continued and has slowed the process of education.

In English/European universities students complete a course of study in about 2 and one-half years. Yet in the US students are required to take four or five years of their life to reach the bachelorrate level of certification.   Distance education attempts to give the student back some of the lecture time for reading and thus speed the process of learning. In this way the student becomes a self-directed learner and is no longer dependent on the pedagogical process of instruction.

In an academic program with distance elements, students are required to do developmental readings in each subject area of a core curriculum prior to participation in a short faculty/student/peer interface class session. The objective is to take advantage of the experience and knowledge of the student and permit each graduate student to become an informed participant in the scheduled class based of cohort session. Following the objectives or essential elements of each course subject in the core, additive reading must be done in all subject areas. To be additive the reading must be eclectic; a few pages from one book, more from another. Students read only those areas which add to the understanding of the essential elements in the syllabus for each subject. It is not the process of reading a number of pages or a number of books, but selective reading to add to their basic knowledge on the subject.

The student may proportion the reading according to their individual needs; for example, those subjects in which the student feels the most informed would require less reading; while other subjects would require more.   The weaker a student is in the subject matter of a particular subject the easier it is to find material which adds to their basic knowledge. Again, this additive material must be related to the essential elements of the course.

Emphasis on Learning
The emphasis is on learning. During developmental readings

the student prepares a learning log covering the material read for each subject in the core. Variant material encountered in the areas of the essential elements should also be addressed. The learning log should include both books and journals. Books should include a few classics and mostly contemporary published during the past ten years. The journal reading should be a current awareness search of appropriate journals during the past three years. Normally, data in journals over three years old has been placed in newly published books.

Counting pages is beneath a graduate student. There is no minimum number of pages because the emphasis is on learning and developing content knowledge in the subject areas. The process is designed to be cumulative. Beginning with the foundational knowledge in the subject areas, eclectic reading should be done which adds to the student's basic understanding of the subject in the areas addressed in the syllabus in the objectives and essential element.

Learning Logs

A Learning Log must be kept in a systematic manner both to bibliographically document the reading and to itemize discovered data which increases the perceptions, reasoning, and learning related to the subject. Most of the learning comes from the reading not the lecture or faculty interface. The faculty is a mentor, a coach; the student is on an academic playing field following a few instructions from the coach. The professor may make a game plan, but the student must make the play by play decision as to the required action.

The learning log should include all new data, both additive and variant, which adds to foundational understanding of the subject. Include in the log additive and variant material: new ideas, concepts, constructs, remote premises, assumptions, operational definitions, subject jargon which add to content/

knowledge or that challenge present understanding. Reading must cover the scope of all the subjects offered in the core session. The student should read selectively in each core subject areas.

Learning Journal

In addition to the learning logs for each subject, the student should provide a summary/analysis of new content gained from the reading by subject. To do this, the student must summarize the new content and analyze how it impacts prior knowledge and present a narrative report which critically assesses the new data. The objective of the narrative report is to produce a degree of acculturation and integration of what has been learned. The process is designed to assist with the assimilation of new ideas into the existing cognitive structure on the subject. Variant material encountered should also be addressed. The narrative report is to be merged into the Learning Journal which is normally the last assignment for each term (semester) for all the subjects taken during the term/semester.

Each student is to keep a Learning Journal to document the process of discovery. Identify ideas, concepts, constructs, etc. from faculty/student interface, peer interface, the syllabus, reading and project assignments and merge this data with the narrative report of the Learning Log. Incorporate the narrative report from the Learning Log with the items which form the Learning Journal. Present the Journal as the final assignment in each term/semester of the Program of Study. The Journal should identify changes related to the student's knowledge and understanding of the subjects. Changes in attitudes, feelings and values which impact conduct should be documented. The emphasis is on learning and change.

Program Learning Chronicle

The Learning Logs for subject readings will be merged as a narrative into the Learning Journal for each term/semester. All learning journals should be combined to form a final document, the Program Learning Chronicle. The Learning Logs and journals reading prepared for all terms/semester should be combined into a master document: Program Learning Chronicle and presented to the Faculty as part of a candidacy evaluation.

A Path to Understanding

Although the emphasis is on learning and ultimately developing a summary document of what was gleaned during the reading process, one may not learn unless the material is understood. The science of hermeneutics is designed to assist the reader in understanding the written material. Chapter three will provide a path to understanding by using interrogatives to guide the process.

Topics Discussed in Chapter Three

Hermeneutic Interrogatives
A Path to Understanding
Hermeneutic Interrogatives
Useful Assumptions in Interpretation
Inductive Study
Observation
Interpretation
Avoidable Dangers
Evaluation and Application
Correlation

INTERROGATIVES AND INTERPRETATION

The Learning Process

Basic questions for hermeneutics, the science of interpretation, relate directly to how one gathers facts, interprets these facts, uses these facts and stores them in the long-term memory. This is the learning process. One should engage written material with at lease five questions: (1) What does the written material say? (2) What does the written material mean? (3) How may the written material be paraphrased to clearly express the author's thoughts? (4) How can my understanding of the written material be supported? And (5) How may what is learned be utilized or applied? These questions interpret the written material at five levels:

1. Memorization
2. Understanding
3. Expressing the thought
4. Providing evidence
5. Applying knowledge

A Path to Understanding

A methodical path is required to understand what is written.

Method is based on the Greek word *methodos,* which literally means "a way or path of transit." Method implies orderly, logical, and effective arrangement and may denote either an abstraction or a concrete procedure. Method is a way of doing things which carefully maintains and fosters conditions conducive to understanding and development.

Hermeneutic Interrogatives

An interrogative is a question, normally, using who, what, when, where, why, and how. To develop the basic context of the writer and the subject at hand, asks formal questions. Both an understanding of written material and an adequate use of printed information may be developed through the interrogatory process.

- WHO is the writer?
- WHERE was the material written?
- WHEN was the material written?
- WHY did the writer write this composition?
- WHAT does the writer say?
- WHAT does the writer mean?
- HOW may the meaning be paraphrased?
- WHERE can collateral evidence be found?
- HOW may the material be applied ?

Hermeneutics, the science of interpretation, is the process by which a reader understands the meaning of an author's words. The meaning may be clarified by considering seven key words:

SEE – Observe the link between subject and object.

INQUIRE – Inquisitiveness is required to find the meaning.

ANSWER – Re-creating the attitude of the writer is a source of answers.

SUMMARIZE – Integrate and summarize to discover the primary message.

EVALUATE – Determine the subject or universal value of the meaning.

APPLY - A true understanding should be applicable to real life.

ASSOCIATE - The meaning of a message must be associated with others in the same work and with data outside the source to develop the ultimate correlation.

Major components of a written passage are:

TERMS – The primary use of a word.

STRUCTURE – The relationship between terms.

GENERAL LITERARY FORMS – The format used to communicate the message.

ATMOSPHERE – The underlying tone or spirit of written material.

Useful Assumptions in Interpretation

- What is read should be an objective body of information.

- A methodical approach is required to gain this information.

- The information communicated by the writer is distinct from the interpreter.

- The interpreter must use an objective approach to extract the writer's true information.

- There is no absolute objectivity or pure induction, because of bias.

- A method that stresses induction should be more impartial and accurate than any other method.

- The method of hermeneutical study should discover the particular facts for sound interpretation.

Inductive Study

Induction is the process of reasoning or drawing conclusions from particular facts or individual cases. In induction one observes a sufficient number of facts, and on the grounds of reason, extends what is true of them to others of the same class, thus arriving at assumptions or general principles. The opposite is true of deduction. One begins with a general truth, and seeks to connect it with some individual case by means of a middle term or class of objects known to be equally connected with both. Thus, one deduces the specific from the general, attributing to the former the distinctive qualities of the latter. The idea of induction is to read out of the text by being an objective observer and a logical interpreter. The process begins with observation.

Observation

Taking into account the above, a basic step is interpretation is observation. This step determines the components of a written document. This step involves perception and is essentially awareness of the process which causes the interpreter to become saturated with the particulars and concerns for the existence of terms and requires definition of terms used in a given context. Observation assists in discovering the structure of a passage through the relations and interrelations between terms (various structural units: phrases, clauses, sentence, paragraph, segment, subsection, section, or division.) Observation identifies the general literary form or forms which cause terms to communicate ideas. Observation opens the interpreter's eye to the atmosphere or underlying tone or spirit of the passage. (Some moods by which a written portion may be characterized: despair, thanksgiving, awe, urgency, joy, humility, or tenderness.)

Interpretation

The next phase is interpretation. One must objectively read out of the text, not subjectively read into the passage. This logical step is to determine the meaning of what is written in relationship to the purpose or objective of the work. Does the author mean exactly what is written? Why was it written? To whom was it written? Was it written to inform, persuade, interpret or answer a question or solve a problem? This requires empathy or projection into the consciousness of the writer. The interpreter must be identified with the writer to understand what is written. This requires the recapturing of the writer's attitudes, motives, thought, and emotions at the time of the writing.

Interpretation is always incomplete, because the interpreter cannot fully reproduce the circumstance of the writer or fully understand the motives of the writer. The basic meaning of the components must be determined through logical steps. This is a definitive phase which corresponds to the function of dictionaries and lexicons. The meaning is not sufficient, the underlying reasons why the statements are made must be determined. There may be a general reason related to the whole of the written work or a particular reason for a particular part. What about the historical situation or the literary context of the writing. The inter-relatedness of facts is the outgrowth of presuppositions and becomes the presupposition of other ideas. The implication of statements is more than the explicit expression. This requires that interpretive questions be applied to the written word. The interpreter must be aware of potential erroneous or inaccurate expositions.

Some possible areas of concern include:

Concern one - Treating a written section as a collection of isolated sentences that may be understood apart from the immediate and broad context.

Concern two - Searching written material with preconceived ideas to substantiate certain personal beliefs;

Concern three - Attempting to rationalize to make written material fit one's bias and thereby eliminate the writer's true purpose;

Concern four - Viewing written material purely from the historical without realizing that all writing contains more than history;

Concern five - Explaining illustrations, for example, as allegories or extended metaphors and, consequently, pressing every detail for some meaning instead of understanding the purpose of the illustration;

Concern six – The reader may see all written material as literally explaining the writer' intent to communicate the true meaning.

Avoidable Dangers

There are other avoidable dangers in interpretation. Some relate to misinterpretation and others to failure to determine the full meaning or seeing more than is actually present in the written passage under consideration.

Avoidable danger one - Viewing what an author writes without considering the time (date) of the writing.

Avoidable danger two - Assuming that an isolated fact is useful without seeing it in the context of the whole work.

Avoidable danger three - View an author's work as a maze of cross-references and not interpret each book in its own right before associating it with the other works of the same author ore other authors.

Avoidable danger four - Seeing a written work as exhaustive rather than seeing it as part of a body of literature.

Avoidable danger five - See the work as great literature rather than its use of literary form to communicate a message.

Evaluation and Application

The third phase of induction is the process of evaluation and application. Written statements need to be evaluated and applied for both education and edification. The worth of each statement must be assessed and its relevance or usefulness determined.

Evaluation should follow interpretation and must not interfere with the process. Evaluation must precede application. Following interpretation, the relevance and worth of the passage is determined with the view of application. Adequate assessment suggests valid application. Application is the final objective of all developmental reading or inductive study and must be preceded by a process of evaluation

Evaluation is both general and specific. The facts may be relevant to a larger study and useful for an intermediate effort. The worth and value of a writer's work is the general step in evaluation. Specifically, the exact worth of a particular portion of writing is necessary because different parts of a work may address specific questions, situations, and consequently, have degrees of relevance and value to support another position or work. The task of evaluation is to distinguish between those facts which are of limited value and those that are timeless and of general use.

When a timeless or general value is determined, a specific use must be analyzed to ascertain whether or not it falls within the scope of a present task or written work. The interpreter must search for a contemporary problem to which the facts are relevant. Application naturally follows. Facts from another source must be applied in an appropriate manner regardless of the consequences.

Correlation

The concluding step of inductive study is correlation. Some correlation occurs during the process of interpretation and application, because it is the natural outgrowth of the examination of written material. In other to develop data useful to build or support a written work, the findings from inductive study must evolve into a synthesized concept that supports the new works thesis or purpose. Facts in a written work must be related to other facts within the same work and facts in other works. The weakest part of inductive study is at this point of generalizations. Most of the interpreter's energy is concentrated on the search for facts and little effort is giving to synthesizing and correlating those facts before they are included in another work. This correlation should be both formal and informal.

An attempt must be made to see another author's work as a whole and determine if it supports the direction of a new work. Even individual chapters of a book should not be interpreted without considering the purpose of the whole book. An effort must be made to the inter-relatedness of facts rather than superficial compartmentalization to fit a new work. This is often called, "the use of proof texts." The ultimate goal of developmental readings is to present additive and variant material in a useful manner.

A Key to Understanding a Subject

Making use of interrogatives facilitates learning and assists with the process of reviewing relevant literature. As one engages the existent literature on a given subject it is necessary to ask questions about the author and the material. When one is comfortable using interrogatives these questions become common place and the review of literature is more productive.

Topics Discussed in Chapter Four

Only a few writers
Key to Understanding a Subject
Basic Research for Writing
A Means to an End
Purpose of a Review
Gathering Data
Before Starting a Review of Literature?
Certain Questions Should be Considered
Enlarging a Writer's Knowledge
Reviews Should Comprise Essential Elements
Understanding the Subject
A Review Surveys Scholarly Articles
Data Worthy of Inclusion
An Overview of the Subject
Similar to Qualitative Research
Every Researchable Idea
Keep in Mind the Purpose
A Narrowing of Focus
A Review Could be Endless

CHAPTER FOUR

REVIEW AND EVALUATION

Only a few writers have sufficient knowledge to write an essay, journal article, or a book without further research. Basic to this research is a review of relevant literature on the subject of concern. For new writers, the literature review is the least valued part of a new composition. These questions should be considered as a writer develops a literature review:

1) What is already known about the subject?

2) What are the gaps in the knowledge of the subject?

3) What areas of further study have been identified by other authors?

4) Who are the significant authors in this area?

5) Is there consensus about among the primary authors on the topic?

6) What aspects of the subject have generated debate?

7) What methods or problems were identified by others studying this field that could impact the new composition?

8) What is the most productive methodology for the review?

9) What is the current status of research on the subject?

10) What sources of information or data were identified that might be useful for the new composition?

Key to Understanding a Subject

The key to understanding published writers in a given field or on a specific subject is a review of relevant material. An author researching for a new composition should not search all the material published, but review and evaluate the relevant literature according to the objectives guiding the composition. Data should be organized around the goals of the new composition.

A review of relevant literature does not describe one piece of literature after another, but should summarize each relevant item and do some critical assessment of material. Use an introduction and conclusion to cover the scope of the review and to formulate the question, problem, or concept for the material chosen to support your new composition by grouping around the objectives of your new composition.

Basic Research for Writing

Authors in preparation to write an essay or book should develop an annotated bibliography as preparation for a full review of literature on the subject. The review should be a record of what has been published on a subject by accredited scholars. In developing the literature review, the author's focus is to determine additive and variant material that will assist in writing the essay, article, or book. It is to assist the writer in structuring the objectives of the new composition. This will allow the reader to be brought up to date on available literature and just how the new composition adds to or has contrasting perspectives or viewpoints than previous writings.

Following a literature review, the author will know the ideas that have been established on a subject and be able to determine an approach to the new composition that can utilize the data already in print. The review should be guided by the purpose of the composition, the problem or issues to be discussed. A descriptive list of material available or book summaries is not sufficient, specific objectives must guide the review that will facilitate the gathering of useable material to support the new composition.

Not to be confused with a book review, a literature review surveys scholarly articles, books and other sources relevant to a particular issue, subject, or theory, providing a description, summary, and critical evaluation of each author's work to clearly understand the significant literature already published on the subject area of the new composition. Now the reviewer knows what others have said and not said and can formulate an original composition based on new knowledge.

Literature Review: A Means to an End

An author's review of literature is a means to an end. Although the review is similar to primary research, it does not present new primary scholarship; this is left to the new composition. An adequate review of relevant literature requires four steps:

1) **Problem formulation**—which topic or field is being examined and what are the relevant issues?

2) **Literature search**—finding materials relevant to the subject being explored determines the scope.

3) **Data evaluation**—determining which literature makes a

significant contribution to the understanding of the subject of the new composition.

4) **Analysis and interpretation**—discussing the findings and conclusions of pertinent literature in terms of the objectives of the new composition.

Purpose of a Review

A literature review may constitute a basic research for writing a book on the subject, the development of an essential chapter in a thesis or dissertation, or may be a self-contained review of a subject. Regardless, the purpose of the review is to:

1) Place each author's work in the context of its contribution to the understanding of the subject under review.

2) Compare the relationship of each work to the others under consideration.

3) Identify ways to interpret or shed light on significant differences between other works.

4) Determine conflicts or data that contradicts other studies.

5) Learn areas of prior scholarship to avoid duplication of effort.

6) Decide what aspects of the problem have and have not been covered in order to determine the direction of the new composition.

7) Place the new composition in the context of existing literature.

Gathering Data

Gathering data is an essential part of writing. When a review of relevant literature permits an author to summarize and explain what others have published, the contrasting perspectives of the new composition may be clearly presented. The review will permit the writer to point out any connections between the sources and identify where one source is built upon a prior work. This permits the new composition to add to the reader's knowledge of the subject.

Before Starting a Review of Literature

Before beginning a review of relevant literature a writer should ask these questions:

1) What is the specific thesis, problem, or research question does my new composition intend to answer?

2) What type of literature review am I conducting?

3) What is the scope of my literature review? What types of publications am I using journals, books, other document, and media data.

4) What discipline or academic field do I need to cover?

5) How good was my information seeking?

6) Has the scope of my search been sufficient to ensure all the relevant material?

7) Has it been narrow enough to exclude irrelevant material? Is the number of sources I've used appropriate for the length of my composition?

8) Have I critically analyzed the literature reviewed? Do I follow through a set of concepts and questions, comparing items to each other in the ways they deal with them? Instead of just listing and summarizing items, do I assess them, discussing strengths and weaknesses?

9) Have I cited and discussed studies contrary to my perspective?

10) Will my literature review be relevant, appropriate, and useful in developing my new composition?

Certain Questions Should be Considered

As one reviews relevant literature certain questions should be considered about each book or article reviewed:

1) Does the author formulated a problem or issue relevant to the new composition?

2) Is it clearly defined? Is its scope, severity, relevance clearly established?

3) Could the problem have been approached more effectively from another perspective?

4) What is the author's perspective: interpretive, critical, or a combination?

5) What is the author's theoretical position: psychological or developmental?

6) What is the relationship between the theoretical and the research perspectives?

7) Is there evidence that the author being reviewed evaluated the literature relevant to the problem or issue?

8) Does the author include literature with variant positions?

9) In an academic study, consider the value of basic components of the study design: population, intervention, and outcome? How accurate and valid are the measurements? Is the analysis of the data accurate and relevant to the research question? Are the conclusions validly based upon the data and analysis?

10) In material written for a popular readership, does the author use appeals to emotion, one-sided examples, or rhetorically-charged language and tone? Is there an objective basis to the reasoning, or is the author merely "proving" what he or she already believes?

11) In what ways does this book or article contribute to an understanding of the problem under study, and in what ways is it useful for the new composition? What are the strengths and limitations?

Enlarging a Writer's Knowledge

Besides enlarging a writer's knowledge about the subject of the new composition, developing a literature review permits the writer to gain and demonstrate skills in two areas:

1) Information Seeking: the ability to scan the literature efficiently, using manual or computerized methods, to identify a set of useful articles and books, 2) Critical Appraisal: the ability to apply principles of analysis to identify unbiased and valid studies.

A literature review must do four things: 1) Be organized around and related directly to the objectives of the proposed new composition, 2) Synthesize results into a summary of what is and is not known, 3) Identify areas of controversy in the literature, and 4) Formulate questions that need further development in the new composition.

Reviews Should Comprise Essential Elements

Literature reviews should comprise the essential elements: 1) An overview of the subject, issues or theory under consideration, along with new data organized around the objectives of the new composition. 2) Division of literature under review into categories of additive and variant material. 3) Explanation of how each concept, construct, theory, or principle relates to the new composition. 4) Conclusions as to the data best considered in support of the objectives of the new composition and a decision as to how the variant material could be presented.

Understanding the Subject

In assessing the work of each published writer, consideration should be given to: 1) Provenance—What are the credentials of the writer? Are arguments supported by evidence? 2) Objectivity—Do the writer's perspective cause disadvantage or harm to somebody or some cause? Is variant data considered or is certain pertinent information ignored to support the writer's point? 3) Persuasiveness—Which of the writer's concepts, constructs, or issues are most/least convincing? and 4) Value—Are the writer's arguments and conclusions convincing? Does the data contribute significantly to an understanding of the subject of the new composition?

A Review Surveys Scholarly Articles

Such a review surveys scholarly articles, books and other

sources relevant to a particular issue, area of research, or theory, providing a description, summary, and critical evaluation of each work. The purpose is to offer an overview of significant literature published on a topic and to assessment its worth and make a judgment as to how the data could be used in an additional composition. The review of literature should not be confused with a book review. The review of a book deals with only one author while a literature review deals with all the significant writers in a given field.

Data Worthy of Inclusion

A literature review is recognition of what has been published on a subject by accredited authors. In developing the review, the purpose is to determine data worthy of inclusion in the new composition. Identify what knowledge and ideas have been gleaned on a subject, and what are the strengths and weaknesses of the sources.   As preparation for writing, the literature review must have a guiding concept, clear objectives, and specific goals to be discussed. It is not just a descriptive list of the material available, or a set of summaries; it should glean useable material that can support a new composition.

An Overview of the Subject

Literature reviews should comprise an overview of the subject, issue or theory under consideration, along with the objectives of the literature review. Works under review should be divided into categories, those in support of and those against a particular position, and those offering alternatives with explanation of how each work is similar to and how it varies from the others. The reviewer must make decisions as to which data is best for the new composition and would make the greatest contribution to the understanding and development of the new composition...

Similar to Qualitative Research

Similar to qualitative research, development of the literature review constitutes an essential aspect of any original composition. The literature review itself, however, does not present new primary scholarship. Some scholars believe that literature searches and subsequent syntheses of related information constitute research per se; however, these actions are only a part of the process. The purpose of a literature review is to glean from published works essential content for a new composition.

The review also assists the writer to describe the relationship of each work to the others under consideration. The review should identify new data and interpret the data to shed light on any gaps in previous research and resolve conflicts amongst seemingly contradictory previous studies. The areas of prior scholarship must be identified to prevent duplication of effort. This also points the way forward for further composition and demonstrates an understanding of previous related research by pointing out agreements and disagreements among the results of various studies. Additionally, the literature may suggest ways of investigating a particular problem and discuss related methodological difficulties

Every Researchable Idea

Every researchable idea involves a number of concepts and complex relationships. In modern society, large data bases have been built around clusters of important problems. Such Internet data bases should be considered an important part of all literature searches. Research attempts to generate new knowledge. A unique synthesis of existing knowledge aids this process and is a necessary first step in any writing project, enabling an author to determine systematically what is already known. Such a search highlights questions that have not been answered. A presentation of such a review should focus on important aspects that directly relate to the objectives of the new composition.

Keep in Mind the Purpose

No doubt long lists of things to look for when reviewing the literature can be constructed. Normally, such lists are not useful. Instead, a writer should simply keep in mind the purpose for reviewing the literature. The findings will assist with refining the objectives of the new composition.   What is discovered about these items is the object of the review effort.

When a problem has been identified and research questions formulated, any review of the literature for a project would include information from the body of literature by experts rather than from popular essays. Such

essays may help develop a general conceptual framework for a project but cannot provide the specific theoretical basis for a new composition.

A Narrowing of Focus

All research problems fit into a larger context. A review should deal first with the general context of the larger issues and relevant theories, then, proceed logically to the specific issues. Such a narrowing of focus leads the assessor to proposed questions. Although the literature review normally follows the presentation of the problem and the purpose of the composition, it forms a foundation for the composition. Consequently, it should clearly support the objectives of the new composition.

A Review Could be Endless

A literature review could be endless; consequently, one should determine the nature and limits of the literature to be reviewed. An adequate search of the literature might begin with several computerized information retrieval systems for published works and other bibliographical data bases designed to reference current published material. Most professions and virtually all disciplines have indexed important articles. The review itself should be focused on the researcher's objectives for the composition. The introduction to a new work should make it clear that the strengths and weaknesses of other research projects have been taken into account. It generally should include citations from the previous five years in addition to any classics in the field. A good review must be more than an annotated bibliography; it ought to be a critical synthesis that prepares a foundation and structure for the new composition.

Reading and Writing go Together

The literature review not only brings additive and variant material into the learning process, much is learned about the writers who engage the subject. The more one knows about the author of a text, the easier it is to comprehend what is written. Knowing the orientation of the writer and the background, philosophy, and purpose of the composition increases the understanding of the written document. The more the reader understands the composition of others, the better writer the reader may become.

Topics Discussed in Chapter Five

COMPOSITION AND HERMENEUTICS

Elusiveness of the Author

A basic difficulty in understanding the written word is not the vagueness of the composition, but the elusiveness of the author. This could be the reason English/European students read authors rather than subjects. The more one knows the author of a text the easier it is to comprehend what is written. Knowing the orientation of the author and the background, philosophy, and purpose of the composition increases the understanding of the written document. For example, one understands a letter from a parent without much difficulty. An unsolicited letter from a stranger giving details about a subject of which one is not already somewhat informed could be perplexing. Yet, the correspondence of two professors is a common academic field interacting on a subject of mutual interest is readily comprehended.

Informal Versus Formal Writing

The science of interpretation primarily relates to formal writing; however, the more the student knows about the process of composition the better the interpretation of written material will be. First, understand the word "composition" simply means with position. Every word, phrase, sentence, paragraph, section and chapter have a proper place in a composition. When all the components of writing are in the proper place or position, the process of understand the meaning and interpreting it to others is simplified. Take a look at both formal and informal writing, because some writers lapse for time to time into an informal mode. To adequately interpret what is written, this must taken into account.

Informal Writing

Informal writing is oral in nature. It is written for the ear. It is casual, simple, and spontaneous and requires little advance preparation. It is unassuming and unconventional. It is a script written to be read aloud or spoken--an oral script. Such writing is basically talking on paper. The emphasis is often lost unless one reads or mouths the words. It is conversational and designed for entertainment or popular reading, such as, novels or plays. TV scripts and TV and radio news are oral scripts, designed to be read aloud and heard with the ear. Emphasis depends on gestures, body language, or inflections of the voice. Informal writing is much easier than the formal, because the ear is a more sensitive sense. Hearing is an outgrowth of the touch, the most personal of senses. Consequently, hearing is a personalized way of touching at a distance. As such, hearing is the most social of the senses and has particular value in the context of informal writing. Informal writing is designed to touch the reader.

Informal Emphasis

The emphasis is often lost unless one reads or mouths the words. The writer uses underlining, bold type, italic, and other oral approaches to emphasize a word or phrase. This function by the writer is a substitute for speaking. Words and phrases are often mouthed or read aloud to determine the emphasis. The oral items above are then used to guide the reader.

Formal Writing

Formal writing is designed to be seen with the eye. It uses Standard English with prescribed or operational definitions. It is sometimes seen as awkward or stiff but always follows a conventional form and style based on the nature of the work and the audience. Since informal writing is talking on paper: formal writing could be characterized as thinking on paper. The emphasis does not depend on the personality of the writer or the variations of voice or gesture. The emphasis is by position or proportion. It is structured to be read by the eye. Since the eye does not see when it moves, only when it stops to focus, punctuation becomes the road signs to stop the eye and enable it to see key words or phrases. By stopping the eye, words and phrases on both sides of the punctuation take on value. The key to formal writing is to keep in mind the words are to be viewed by the eye not heard by the ear.

Emphasis by Position and Proportion

Words and phrases are emphasized by the position in the sentence. Sentences are emphasized by their position in the paragraph and paragraphs are emphasized by their position in the article or chapter. The most emphatic position is at the end of the sentence. The second most emphatic position is at the beginning. The same holds true for the sentences in a paragraph and for paragraphs in a composition.

Value is awarded to paragraphs and chapters by both position and proportion. Those last and first have position for emphasis. The others must be emphasized by size and proportion. Those paragraphs and chapters, which fall between the first and the last, must be given size according to their position.

Paragraphs lost in the middle of the composition or chapters stuck in the middle of a book, must be larger in size and more carefully written to get the attention of the reader and send the message of value for the contents. The closer these elements are to the first or last position the less the size. The closer to the middle the larger they must be to hold their value in the eye of the reader.

Diagnosing Writing Problems

The problems in writing create difficulties in adequate interpretation of what is written. Poor writers are not easily understood. The better the writer the easier it is to understand and interpret the meaning of written material. If the interpreter knows the normal pitfalls of writing, this fact can be observed when a writer lapses into poor style. Style is simply the way a writer puts thoughts and words together. Poor writing is poor thinking. Good and logical writing is easily understood.

Examine - To Diagnose the Problem.

What is the writer's problem? An interesting person may be a dull, foggy writer because he does not consider the basic principles of clarity. Weakness must be recognized and corrected before a superior writing style can emerge. Most poor writers can find their faults in this list:

Wordiness: Readers are busy. They will not take time to figure out complicated vocabulary or plow through unnecessary words. Long, complicated words were constructed to think with, not to be used in basic communication.

Poor Planning: It does not matter how fast or carefully you travel; if you are on the wrong road, the destination will not be reached. Planning time is as important as writing time. Poor planning triggers bad tone and poor organization. Before you write, think about what you are to say, plan how to say it, and organize your thoughts before starting the first draft.

Bad Organization: Work out an outline. Otherwise, there will be sentences and paragraphs going off in several directions. The lack of outline and structure is a serious writing weakness. Effective writing follows a logical and orderly progression of ideas. The main points are determined through planning. These are organized to present points most logically to the reader.

Weak Start: Beginning without an outline, poor writers go into a writing shell and strain for words and ideas. They lose the simple conversational quality essential to good writing and become overly concerned with form, grammar, and punctuation during the first draft. The mechanics can be improved during revision. Naturally, a good title and outline helps the writer to have a good beginning. Revision can and will make the writing more effective.

Sentences: Sloppy sentences are robbers of clarity. A good sentence conveys the exact meaning without embellishment. Sentences should be short unless the writer has mastered balance and other subordinating techniques. Beware of dangling, misplaced, and pyramiding modifiers, fuzzy statements, big words, passive voice, and topsy-turvy structure.

Transitions: Paragraphs are the major units of writing. Although the unadorned declarative sentence is a major accomplishment, the sentence must be properly placed into a paragraph. The sentence flow of long paragraphs must be smooth and the idea relationship clear. Remember that a paragraph develops one idea. These basic units of composition are linked with words or idea bridges, which help in the transition from one idea to the next. The reader must understand the relationship of ideas from paragraph to paragraph to understand when the writer has finished with one idea and is ready to move to another.

Words and Tone: Composition is a substitute for personal contact. The language, approach, and tone used should be polite and acceptable to the reader. Use short, familiar words; most people want information in simple form. A poor choice of words, a misplaced punctuation, or a twist of a phrase can cut deep into a reader's sensibilities, defeating the purpose of the composition. Watch for punctuation, style, spelling, and grammar; breakdowns here confuse the reader and distort meaning. When mechanics, word choice or tone go astray, so does emphasis and coherence. Revision is vital to correct these weaknesses. Reading the composition aloud helps. The ear picks up some things the eye cannot. The use of a good dictionary helps, too!

The interpreter's personal writing problems are also a hindrance to good interpretation. One who understands grammar, sentence structure, emphasis, etc. is better equipped to interpret written work. To improve personal ability to interpret written material, become a better writer.

What is your basic writing problem? Perhaps you have more than one weakness. There is no advantage knowing about the weakness unless it is strengthened. These weak aspects of your journalistic skill should be strengthened by immediate action.

Launch a self-improvement effort immediately. Read. Talk with others. Examine closely the work of good journalists. Work out a plan of self-improvement. Do some work in weak areas several days until you have developed a habit of self-improvement. Do not worry about weaknesses. Strengthen them. Some will always remain. The important thing is that you recognize and improve at your weakest points. Do not let weaknesses hinder you from writing. Rewriting can improve and make almost any manuscript acceptable. Of course, it may have to be reworked several times, but you can do it. Just get started! Follow the TPO formula (think, plan, organize) before you write. This plan is based on some aspects of ancient rhetoric: invention, disposition, and elocution.

Aristotle identified the first three steps in the rhetorical process as invention, arrangement, and style, but he added three aspects to bring credibility to the author: *ethos, pathos,* and *logos.* Ethos is a demonstration of who he author knows of the subject that influence the reader to accept the author's work as believable. Pathos is a construct relative to the author presenting a topic in a way that evokes strong emotions in the reader. Logos has to do with logical reasoning and objectivity in constructing a written document. Although these concepts are from the classical world of centuries ago, they remain good guideposts for writers.

Creative writing is certainly a process of invention, but there are other elements of writing that are germane to this text; namely, *revising, rewriting, proof reading, re-wording,* and the list goes on and on, but the element of "time" is the limiting factor as the diagram below shows.   Always if there were more time one could do a better, but reality is that there is never enough time to continue writing a composition over and over. One must do the best they can in the time that they have. This includes time for proofing and revising.

EW = <u>T P O</u>
WRRRR/RRR
[time]

Effective Writing = Think – Plan –Organize (TPO)
Write – read, revise, rewrite, revise/ revise
                                                TIME

Think - To Invent A Subject.

An inevitable act of writing is finding something to say. The what, why and who are the first hurdles. What are you going to write? Why are you writing? What do you know about the subject? What information will you need from other sources? Who is your reader? Facts to support ideas and examples to explain ideas must come from somewhere, whether from your head, from research, or from a combination of both. Classical writers called this the process of invention. Actually, it means to find. The use of gray matter is essential to inventing a subject and finding something to say. There is no substitute for thinking.

What are you going to write?

A definite aim is essential to writing. Actually write down what the definite aim is before proceeding to choose a subject. The field must be narrowed to the specific aspect that can be covered in the proposed length of the composition.

Zeroing in on a specific subject assists the writer in several ways. It provides a starting place for reading and research. It guides in the developing of an outline to insure against sidetracks. Specifying a subject also helps identify the reader. This is a basic step in good journalism.

Why are you writing?

Decide! Writing to impress others with your knowledge will not produce a good composition. Write to be read. Keep in mind the three basic objectives of writing: (1) to inform, (2) to persuade, and (3) to interpret. Choose the proper one. Are you writing to arouse interest, influence attitudes, solve problems, implement progress, or evaluate results?

Should your goal be to inform state facts objectively and add to the reader's knowledge of the subject. To do this, a judgment must be made as to the present knowledge the reader may possess. When your goal is to persuade, attractive arguments and reasons should be used to stir the reader to decision. When you wish the reader to make up his own mind, write to interpret by analyzing facts and giving opinions.

Knowing why a composition is being presented helps the writer deal with specific issues. This improves the possibilities of good communication with the reader and lessens the chances of misinterpretation.

What do you know about the subject?

Why was this subject selected? Do you know a great deal about the field? Serious thinking is required at this point. To gain the reader's confidence, there must be no mistakes. The writer must have confidence in his knowledge of the subject. This is where he gets the authority to write, select details, use examples, and subject his work to the critical eye of process analysis.

What information will you need from other sources? Determining your limitations is the starting point. Research is the only way to compensate for prior lack of knowledge. Consider both primary sources and secondary sources. Talk and write to people. Read books, magazines, and papers. Interview, run tests, survey what others have done on the subject. Use your own library, the public library, and the libraries of educational institutions in the area.

Research until you have the facts to support your ideas. Think of examples to explain your ideas. Gather facts and list them in support of each idea or recommendation. No writing can be convincing without backup data.

Think of examples to explain your ideas. Examples perk up a paper and turn a dull subject into an interesting composition. Facts show a writer's research; examples show his imagination.

Plan - To Arrange Ideas.

Next, based on your reading, list the ideas to be used in the composition. This list should include questions the reader may ask and ideas you think are important. From these questions, list in priority order which facts should be used to answer questions or support a point of view. This gives you the main ideas for the composition and provides a basis for organization of ideas into an outline for writing.

When ideas to be included in the composition are gathered, the next step is to find an effective order in which to present the information. Ancient writers called this "disposition." It was a process of ordering or arranging material. Disposition actually means, "to arrange." It is the business of deciding on the relevance and value of key facts, arranging them in groups and ordering those groups to achieve the desired effect on the readers.

Who are the readers?

Material cannot be properly arranged without a knowledge of the readers. Who are they? What are their backgrounds? How much do they know about the subject? How will they use the information? How much time will they give to the composition? Are they likely to be receptive?

What message form will you use?

The message form has a great deal to do with how you write. The reader and his time combine to choose the message form. Will it be a letter, a report, a memorandum, an article, a telegram, or a book? Regardless of the form your message takes, the objective remains the same: communicate ideas concisely and clearly!

Organize - To Present Facts.

First, the specific purpose or thesis for the composition must be stated. The thesis has three elements: What, why, and who. What are you writing about? Why are you writing (inform, persuade, or interpret)? Who is your reader? The answer to these three questions provides a clear thesis. The order may be why, who, what in the final statement of the thesis.

Chapters, sections, paragraphs, thoughts must be presented in an organized format or the composition will not make sense. Readers react the same way to poorly organized writing as they would to the scenes of a drama being presented out of order. When thoughts are hard to follow, the reader gives up.

Trouble with organization is usually caused by a writer attempting to cover too much or because he cuts detail too fine. In such case the writer probably has limited himself to an outline of Roman numerals and capital letters. The outline is incomplete because he failed to plan the development and the presentation of detail. Some writers have too few headings; others have too many. Without an adequate outline, there will most likely be poor transition between sections, paragraphs, and sentences. Important ideas will be buried in tangled thoughts and unbalanced structure.

There are several ways to avoid such pitfalls. Professional writers fit their ideas into one of several organization plans. After listing ideas in the previous chapter, you are ready to choose an organization plan.

Time - the basic order is chronological.

Major topics - name your major topics in the first paragraph, then write about them in that order.

Simple to complex - bring a reader along gradually from easy to difficult ideas.

Least important to most important - work the subject toward a climax.

Space - if you are writing about land, offices, department, classes, use the space plan.

Problem-solving - A popular plan for fact-finding and study groups. State the problem in a brief sentence and propose possible solutions.

Reason - Here you state an opinion or point of view and then give reasons why you support it.

Question & Answer - Use to explain a program, procedure, operation, or system to a large audience.

Format for a Formal Outline

The key to outlining a book is to organize down to the "idea" or paragraph level.   Since a paragraph is one idea fully developed, the "idea" level is the paragraph-level. Do not begin to write until you have organized your ideas in a logical sequence. The outline below is more detailed than most writers would need for an essay of short article; however, for a textbook or a major publication ,a detailed outline would be needed.

First Main Idea.
A. Fact supporting this idea.
1. Sources leading to A.
2. Important item relating to A.
   a) Support for 2.
   b) Additional support for 2.
      (1). Item relating to b).
      (a). Item relating to (1).
      (b). Second item relating to (1).
         (2).   Another item relating to b).
B. Another significant fact supporting main idea.
1. Sources leading to B.
2. Important item relating to B.
3. Etc.

C. Etc.

Second Main Idea.
A.   Etc.
B.   Etc.

Write - To Express Yourself.

When you have worked through invention and disposition (the THINK - PLAN - ORGANIZE sequence), you know what to say and where in the composition to say it. The remaining act of writing is simply to say it, to put your thoughts into the most telling prose you are capable of writing.

The Roman writers with oration in mind called this step elocution or to speak out plainly. This is essentially what is meant by the word "expression." The time has come to simply express yourself clearly. Put your ideas and thoughts into words. You know what you want to say and where you want to say it. There is nothing to worry about except expressing your thoughts on paper.

Remember you are writing on paper, not eternal bronze. Just put down the first sentence as it comes to mind. Complete the first paragraph. It may all be omitted in revision, but you cannot have a second paragraph until you have written the first. No one will publish it as it stands in the first draft. That is what revision is all about, but you have to have a draft to revise!

Most professional writers make a quick draft, often without giving it their best effort. They simply put their thoughts on paper knowing they can be sharpened up during revision. Even the most accomplished professional will never be satisfied with the effectiveness of a first draft composition. It is simply a first try. This means there are no good writers, but there are good re-writers.

The think-plan-organize sequence brings the writer nearly halfway through the writing process before the first draft. Do not worry about mechanics. Don't worry about form and structure. All this can be perfected later. Just put your thoughts on paper. Write to express your ideas. It is your idea, your pen, your words, and your draft. Do it your way! Let it sound like you. Permit your own style to come through.

Have you tried writing on index cards? What about colored paper? Perhaps ruled paper is best for you. Maybe you prefer to peck away on an old typewriter. Could grade school penmanship be your bag? Do you prefer a tape recorder, so you can write aloud? It is your choice. Do it your way. The way you feel comfortable. With adequate preparation and a comfortable place, you should be able to write without worry.

The best place to start is always at the beginning, but you have done that. The think-plan-organize sequence was the starting place. Now you are not bound to any particular sequence. The outline is filled with good ideas. Look for a few key ideas. Then pick any key point on the outline and develop it, using the facts and examples gathered during research. Soon one sentence will follow another and you will be on your way to a first draft.

Of course, you were told not to worry, but you should worry a little. All writing needs a good beginning. You may start your composition at a key place in the outline, but eventually you must write the first sentence. The first paragraph(s) are important because they suggest to the reader what he can expect. Also, a good opening paragraph helps the writer produce a quick and more effective first draft by igniting a chain of ideas and setting a mood of confidence.

Revise - To Improve Style.

Style is the total effect of writing. It is achieved by the ideas, the organization, the paragraphs, the sentences, the words, all working together harmoniously to express the personality and thoughts of the writer. Style demonstrates the way a writer thinks and expresses their thoughts.

A negative reaction to a writer is a reader's expression of style recognition. From the reader's viewpoint, the composition is disliked or rejected because the reader does not appreciate the writer's style. When one dislikes a writer's style, he simply dislikes the way the writer thinks, expresses himself, his choice of words, sentence patterns, paragraph sequence, or transitions. Style then is usually recognized by negative reaction.

Revision gives the writer opportunity to practice this negative aspect of style recognition. Anything the writer dislikes must be changed and placed into acceptable form or style. Actually, a first draft is an inadequate expression and shows the writer certain areas where he lacks knowledge. When anyone considers a first draft a finished product, he does not understand the basic elements of writing.

The importance of revision cannot be overestimated. It is the difference between good writing and bad writing. Revision is not an unnecessary nuisance; it is an essential element of writing. No composition is complete without revision. Unrevised, it is only a draft, and a draft is not a completed product.

Revision requires the writer to switch roles. He must become an editor and a critic. It is more than flipping through the pages checking for sentence sense and obvious errors. The writer must stop being the creator and become the composition critic. This is the writer's role during revision.

Adequate revision gives the writer opportunity to judge the composition and prepare for reader reaction. More importantly, the writer has a chance to see his best ideas at work and has the privilege of revising and rearranging these ideas so they have the desired prominence and effect.

Always leave space in the first draft for revision, leave room to work between the lines. This means you should double-space or triple-space the first draft. When space is not left for revision, a writer may be tempted to make another draft instead of revising the original. A writer is always better off using second draft time revising the first draft. Leaving space to revise is an important aspect of writing.

Do not revise immediately after writing the first draft. There needs to be a fallow period when the manuscript is forgotten. A composition can never be adequately criticized immediately after a draft is finished. The writer is too close to the problem to be objective. Remember the role change in revision. The writer is now an editor and a critic. Put the first draft away immediately. Do not tinker with it. Transfer your mind to another project and forget about the composition. Later you can be more objective.

It is best to write straightforward during the first draft, pausing as little as possible to make changes. It takes a special mindset to do this, but it is a more efficient way to express yourself on paper. No matter how well the draft is prepared, no one can anticipate all the traps and special problems that may occur in a manuscript. When the cooled-off draft is picked up for revision, the writer must brace himself for a shock. It may be worse than expected, especially at the beginning. This is no cause for discouragement. This is a part of the process!

The first few pages or paragraphs should be viewed carefully. The worst writing usually comes at the beginning, because the writer was trying to get the feel of the composition. The other place to look for special difficulties is just before the end. In a long work, careful revision is needed anywhere the writer was tired or bored. When the writer's energy slackens, he begins to write mechanically from notes. This cramps his style. Anything can happen. Careful revision is essential to effective composition.

Revision must be orderly. It is not enough to read through the draft looking for something to change. There must be a plan. Try this one: (1) cut away the fat, (2) read aloud for content, (3) again read aloud for style, (4) watch for the common errors usually repeated. Each writer needs a self-improvement plan that includes a personal errors list. When the same mistake is repeated, it should go on an errors list. Use this list as a final step in revision. Try not to make the same mistake again.

Revision Plan

1. **Cut out the fat.** Wordiness is a constant difficulty with all writers. Vigor can be added to a style simply by cutting out all words unnecessary to effectively communicate the idea. Think of a telegram. Weigh each word, because each word affects style. Cut not only needless words, but unnecessary sentences and even poor paragraphs that do not contribute to the sense of the manuscript.

Go through the entire draft marking out unnecessary words. Use a wide felt pen to block out words, and phrases so completely that nothing remains to distract as the manuscript is read again. Remember, look especially at the first few paragraphs or pages. The worst writing is probably there.

Check the introduction. It may not make sense now. It may be necessary to cut a big slice off the beginning. The third paragraph on the second page may contain the kind of beginning that could capture reader interest and insure consideration of the composition. Keep this in mind as you cut out the fat!

2. **Read aloud for content.** Reading the manuscript aloud is important, because the ear can detect errors the eye misses. Read aloud first for content. Read the trimmed-down draft aloud slowly listening to the sense of the composition. The fallow period and the cutting down should change the manuscript sufficiently to permit objectivity. Ask honest, critical questions; it is being read for content. Is the main point of each paragraph clear? Is the idea obvious? How is the transition? Has that been said before? Is it logical? Can it be simplified? Does it need more detail or an example? When a question of clarity arises, begin to simplify at once. Confusion usually coincides with unnecessary complexity. When something seems unclear ask, "What do I really mean here?" The answer will simplify, clarify, and revise the problem passage.

Check the manuscript to see that each main point of the organizational outline is clearly expressed. Seek help from a friend. Ask that the composition be summarized by its major points. If a friend misses the main points, critics certainly will see the problem. Anytime the writer has to say, "What I meant was . . . ," something is missing or complicated about the manuscript.

3. **Read aloud again for style.** The manuscript has been repaired to insure sense and clarity, now it must be checked for rhythm. Listen for sentences with a sedative or washboard effect. Watch for verbal echoes and any unnecessary play on

words. Cutting and revising may have caused difficulties of style that were not present before. Always observe punctuation as the manuscript is read aloud. Cutting may have left a series of similar short sentences that need attention. Listen for the complex as well as the over-simplified. Keep at least one ear open for pretentious, pompous, formal style that does not sound natural.

Remember, style is the way a writer expresses personal thoughts and should be recognized as the writer's own vocabulary. Eliminate anything that does not sound natural. If it is not natural to the normal thinking of the writer, it probably will not be clear to the reader.

4. **Error list.** Finally, get out your error list. Remember, those same mistakes made each time - those little notes written on the side of each paper by a patient and helpful professor. There is no better check than the use of a personally accumulated error list.

Forewarned is forearmed! Following each typing, the manuscript must be copy-read for typographical errors. Blaming mistakes on a typewriter or typist can never erase mistakes on a manuscript. The writer is responsible regardless of who does the typing. Read the typist's work twice. Read once for sense and read again for word accuracy. The second time ignore the sense, check words for spelling and transposed letters. There are no typos on a manuscript that is complete; typographical mistakes are simply errors.

Always make a back-up disc and a hard copy of the manuscript. It is good insurance against the U.S. Mail's failure to deliver. In addition, reading a manuscript in the pre-published form is valuable to the writer. Copy-editing or publishers' proofreading will usually add to the writer's errors list.

A systematic approach to revision gives the writer control over the writing process. Augmented by a personal error list, this approach guarantees improvement. Application of these steps makes good sense. The world is overcrowded with poor writers. Ignore these techniques and you remain with the crowd. Use them and become the writer you want to be.

Checklist for writing and revising the first draft

I.   Leave space for revision.
II.   Wait at least 24 hours before beginning revision.
III.   Expect the worst writing at the beginning.
IV.   First, cut out unnecessary words.
V.   Next, read aloud for content.
VI.   Read aloud again for style.
VII.   Check draft against errors list.
VIII.   Proofread at least twice: once for sense, once for individual words.
IX.   Accept responsibility for typographical errors.
X.   Be proud of your composition!

Revise - To Sharpen Sentences.

The sentence has an effective place in the process of style. A workable technique to manage the writing of a sentence is almost nonexistent. A variety of subjected human variables account for this scarcity. Yet without these variables there would certainly be no eloquent style, for style springs from such individual sources. A few common sense guidelines do exist that can point to areas of improvement in the management of sentences. The stylistic instinct must be awakened. This is the instinct, which comes with rhetorical gifts, which usually result from a great deal of reading. Vast reading experience seems to improve verbal aptitude, and naturalness grows that improves word selection and a sense of speech rhythm. This improves sentence control and emphasis. People who read regularly are unafraid to write. They feel at home in the world of words.

Perhaps a review of the copying technique would be helpful. This is an instant reading experience that has a teaching value. Simply choose an author you like and a subject of interest. Select a paragraph or two, which you consider to be well written. The passage should be about twelve sentences in length.

Observe the structure of the paragraph and the four paragraph essentials. A paragraph must (1) be founded on a topic sentence, (2) develop an evident progress of thought, (3) orient the reader to the thought process by use of connective and transitional signposts, and (4) make the reader aware of the place of the paragraph in the larger composition by some indication of function.

After the paragraph structure is clear, move to the next step. Read the material aloud, listening to the stages in the paragraph structure. Now, you are ready for the copying process, which should quickly give you insight into the writer's technique of his ideas in sentences and groups of sentences. On the surface, this process may seem unnecessary, but it is a sure way to develop an instinct for prose style and build naturalness into your writing.

The copying technique works this way. Read each sentence slowly aloud as you copy it by hand noting its pattern of emphasis and rhythm. Then copy the entire passage again trying to hear the sentences together in groups of two or three. By the completion of the exercise, you should have the rhythm and scheme of emphasis in your mind. The point of the whole process is learning to sense what sentences sound right. This can awaken the stylistic instinct. Watch for rhythmic monotony in sentences. The elementary cause of this monotonous style is the sedative and the washboard effect in sentences. These often occur together in the work of inexperienced writers.

A series of sentences of the same length create the sedative effect on the reader. The monotonous sameness has the same effect as counting sheep. A bored reader, if he continues at all, will not understand. If two sentences of the same length appear together, do something to make the next one longer or shorter. Another way to break up the effect is to reduce one or two less important sentences to subordinate or dependent clauses with an important sentence serving as the main clause. These longer sentences will break the sameness.

A series of sentences beginning with their subjects creates a washboard effect and is a major cause of monotonous style. Inexperienced writers give their readers considerable discomfort with this weak sentence sequence. The cure for the washboard is the same as the sedative. As a rule, do not write more than two consecutive sentences beginning with subjects. Parallelism is to find elements that are mobile, such as adverbs, phrases, and subordinate clauses. Move these to the beginning of the sentence and break the washboard rhythm.

Simple and compound sentences are specialized sentences. A simple sentence has one independent clause. The compound sentence is two simple or two complex sentences joined by such words as *and, but, or, nor,* or *for.*

A strategy of sentence variety must consider the sentence used most often in writing: a complex sentence. Remember that the complex sentence has one independent clause and one or more subordinate or dependent clauses. The flexibility of the subordinate clause allows the complex sentence more variety of rhythm and emphasis than a simple or compound sentence. A skillful use of the sentence permits a reader to go through a series of sentences without sensing s sameness. You can spot complex sentences by the words that introduce the dependent thought or connect the two clauses, such as *since, although, after, as,* and *because.*

You may come across the terms *loose* and *periodic* sentences, which describe the emphasis of the major elements. If a sentence has the main idea at the beginning, it is a loose sentence. If the idea is at the end it is periodic. The periodic sentence is more emphatic than the loose sentence, but the strongest positions within the sentence remain at the beginning and the end. The best word order for a sentence is the natural one: subject - verb - object. It is the combination that will keep you out of trouble.

Openers-openers attract attention and arouse interest; consequently, titles and leads are important to composition. They are the first words the reader sees and are the basis of his decision to continue reading. Openers are crucial to good writing.

Focus on titles and leads after the first draft. Jot down ideas as you write, but a completed draft provides better possibilities. A phrase in the third paragraph or a sentence in the fifth paragraph with a little polish may make a good title or a catchy lead.

Titles-a good title is accurate and specific, clear and concise, lively and original. Different methods provide titles:

Subject--a subject may be unusual and a sample description makes an attractive title.

Alliteration--the same first syllable sounds can fix the reader's wandering glance.

Opposing Ideas--Strong contrast between opposing ideas makes readers pause: "The Truth about Lying!"

Parodies of Well-Known Sayings: "Hitch your star to a wagon."

Made-up or Unusual Words--You can count on the offbeat to stop readers.

Single Noun--Many times only one word can tell the story vividly.

Active verbs--a strong active verb arouses reader interest.

Informative--Popular are titles beginning with how, why, where, what, story of, future of, truth about, because they appeal to the reader to enlarge his knowledge-- "Why Churches Die?"

Questions--Reserve the questions for a subject that has wide interest-- "Why Wait 'til Sunday?"

Prepositional Phrase--A prepositional phrase, for some reason, sticks in the readers' mind-- "From Here to Eternity."

Writers should abandon terms in vogue at the turn of the last century, and restore the human quality to their composition. Hackneyed phrases are not eloquent, but worn-out; not a badge of superior learning, but proof of a writer's need for a refresher in elementary composition.

Review- To Make Final Touches

After-You-Write Check List

The Message: Is the subject stated clearly? Does the subject advance steadily? Are the facts correct? Have you included enough data? Have you included too much data?

The Reader: Are there words or expressions that can be misinterpreted? Is the actor or action clear? Have you cut out superfluities? Have you accentuated the positive? Is the tone polite and courteous?

The Treatment: Is the writing concise? Are main ideas emphasized?

Retype - To Produce Final Copy

Publish - To Distribute

Accept responsibility for your work! As you become a better writer, you automatically become a better interpreter of the writings of others. The two go together. Reading and writing are two sides of the same coin. Heads you are the creator of a composition. Tails you are the reader interpreting the message of another writer. Many of the skills overlap. As a writer interprets the work of others, there is a learning process that improves both writing skills and interpretive expertise.

Understanding the Instructional Methodology

The ability to read and understand a subject is central to a quality education. The better one becomes as a reader and a writer, the easier it becomes to study. Understanding the technical nature of writing and the structure of a composition greatly facilitates the learning during the time spent in study. Understanding the instructional methodology and using study time wisely greatly facilitates learning.

Topics Discussed in Chapter Six

Instructional Methodology
Course Textbook Laboratory Design
Other Study Methodologies

CHAPTER SIX
THEORETICAL AND TAXONOMICAL CONSTRUCTS

Instructional Methodology

Theoretical and taxonomical constructs governing the instructional methodology and the tutorial procedures of English/European universities is based on a mature understanding of what is read. The ability to read and understand subjects is central to a quality education. The Europeans think and write in paragraphs, while Americans do well to compose a complete sentence. Americans read books, Europeans read authors and subjects. It is a totally different approach to reading and writing. Understanding how this classical education system works is part of knowing hermeneutics, the science of interpretation.

The tutorial procedures used for centuries in the educational process at these universities was not fully codified until 1989. Hollis L. Green, ThD, PhD, and the faculty of Oxford Graduate School did extensive work to identify and describe the tutorial techniques of the University of Oxford. A comprehensive review of the mass of literature created by both the faculty and alumni of the university, together with personal interviews of faculty, students, and alumni, permitted Oxford Graduate School to codify, in a small way, some of the procedures that have been used. Understanding these procedures will greatly improve the techniques used in the science of interpretation of written material.

Data gathered from university sources has been tempered with European methodology and American educational practices in an effort to place the procedures in a context for the education of adults. The instructional and tutorial procedures used by Oxford Graduate School faculty are a result of efforts to adapt these procedures to the context of the American student. Consequently, the methodology and the andragogical/synergogical tutorial procedures of Oxford Graduate School form a model created from adaptations derived from an eclectic process

Course Textbook Laboratory Design

Among the several designs, the Course Textbook Laboratory Design is most descriptive of the methodology. The design creates classroom dynamics for the student doing faculty directed study. Authors of the various texts are viewed as persons. The author of the primary text is considered the principal source of course content. Authors of the secondary texts serve as the two best informed members of the class who will agree and disagree with the principal source. Authors of the general bibliography form the balance of the class. The student's present knowledge of the subject matter becomes a source of interaction with the authors to complete classroom dynamics of this sixteen-step plan.

The process places the learner inside the dynamics of an interactive learning environment. Interacting with the authors provides a hands-on training for analyzing and interpreting the written material. By dealing with additive and variant material the learner develops insights to the writers thinking and writing techniques. The following 16 steps can open a wide door to understanding both reading and writing.

(1) **Using the course description**, select a primary text and two secondary texts for the course. These are to be approved by your Faculty Advisor and the Faculty designated for the course.

(2) **Develop a brief bibliograph**y of three-to-six volumes related specifically to the course of study. In some select cases, a general bibliography of the field of study would be acceptable.

(3) **Make an initial evaluation** of the primary and secondary texts. Using only the title, table of contents, preface, introduction, publisher's blurb, glossary, forward, or afterward, write a one-page explanation of what you consider to the purpose of each text.

(4) **Read the primary and secondary texts** carefully and write a brief paragraph on each chapter identifying the major themes and/or elements.

(5) **Select from the primary text** the chapter most foundational to the study as described in the course description. Defend the choice in writing. Study the selected chapter noting what seems important. Write a summary/analysis or sentence outline of this chapter.

(6) **Survey the secondary texts** for additional material which supports the data from the foundational chapter. Delineate this additional material.

(7) **Survey the secondary texts** for material which does not agree with the data in the foundational chapter. Delineate this variant material.

(8) **Review the additional bibliography** for additive and variant material with relation to the foundational chapter of the primary text. Delineate this additional material which supports the primary text and that which is at variance.

(9) **Select the chapter in the primary text** which is most conclusive or implemental to the course. Defend this choice. Write a summary/analysis or sentence outline of this chapter.

(10) **Survey the secondary texts** for additional material which supports the data from the conclusive/implemental chapter. Delineate this material.

(11) **Survey the secondary texts** for material which does not agree with the data in the conclusive/implemental chapter of the primary text. Delineate this additional material which supports the primary text and that which is at variance.

(12) **Review the additional bibliography** for additive and variant material with relation to the conclusive/implemental chapter of the primary text. Delineate this additional material which supports the primary text and that which is at variance.

(13) **Select from the primary text** the chapter most applicable to your life and/or career. Defend the choice in writing. Study the selected chapter noting what is important. Write a summary/analysis or sentence outline of this chapter.

14) **Write a one page explanation** of ways you may use what you have learned from this study in your professional and/or personal life.

(15) **Evaluate the texts and the bibliography**. Write a brief evaluation of the primary and secondary texts noting their

strengths and weaknesses. Given the opportunity, how would you improve the bibliography you used in this course?

(16) **Compose an examination** of 50 questions covering this study. Write 20 true and false questions and indicate the correct answer. Write 10 fill in the blank questions and designate the correct answer. Write 10 matching questions and indicate the correct answer. Write 10 short essay questions and write a paragraph or two to answer each. Be balanced, complete, clear, and specific.

When the 16 assignments are completed, submit the primary text and the secondary texts together with* the assignments to: the Professor of record.

Other Study Methodologies

Other study methodologies based on this design may be found in the text Philosophy of Adult Education. Presently nine (9) formal procedures are utilized as instructional methodology by the faculty. Other designs are used informally to judge performance skills and to clarify attitudes as a significant aspect of social effectiveness. The primary methods are:

1) **Seminar Format** for courses requiring specific competency assessment for further study.

2) **Colloquium Design** for courses requiring general competency assessment.

3) **Tutorial Methodology** used for individuals and small groups requiring guidance in a particular area of instruction.

4) **Study Group Design** for presenting content that requires students to learn facts and deduce principles for application.

5) **Participant Teaching Design** when the subject matter can be subdivided as a pre-study assignment and the content taught to other members of the class.

6) **Course Textbook Laboratory Design** to create classroom dynamics. In this methodology students view authors as persons and classify a bibliography based on a course description as primary and secondary texts and general bibliography. The student interacts with the authors dealing with additive and variant material to complete the acquisition of course content and produce data to be reviewed by the professor. (Described above)

7) **Textbook Project Design** builds on the knowledge students acquired in the Course Textbook Laboratory format. The acquisition of information is used as research in preparation for a significant writing assignment.

8) **The Historical/Theoretical Process** to enhance know-ledge of subject matter. The student develops historical and theoretical research skills by developing an annotated bibliography and a reading log of specific material.

9) **The Content Synthesis Process** is used to develop know-ledge of course content not previously studied. Methodology is designed to develop research skills, to acquire data, to develop a synoptic abstract of a particular field of study or a summary analysis of specified material as preparation for research and literature review.

A Tool for Communicating Data

The study methodologies are designed to facilitate the learning process because that is the goal of all education. However, when one gathers additive and variant material and summarizes the material into a new document, the problem becomes one of communication; how best to present the data to others. In the case of new discoveries and conclusions, from testing hypothesis or just developing basic assumptions to the point of making a judgment, the use of statistics at times becomes a tool to communicate what one has learned.

Topics Discussed in Chapter Seven

Communication Tool
Language and Graduate Studies
Behavior as a Statistic
Functions of Statistics
Summarizing
Describing
Summarizing
Experimenting
Counting
Measurements
Nominal Scale
Ordinal Scale
Interval Scale
Ratio Scale
Hypothesis Testing
Decision Model

STATISTICS VIEWED AS A LANGUAGE

Communication Tool

Statistics is a tool for simple and effective communication of information, especially new information. In academic and professional pursuits, one must learn the methodology of both understanding what is presented in statistical format and develop the ability to communicate personal research findings in a statistical manner that is understand by others. Statistics can be compared to using a microscope, telescope, overhead projector, videotape, film, textbook, or a computer. The process is not complicated; it is sophisticated. Once the rules and regulations are understood the process is simplified. A researcher makes a decision about the best way to present quantitative and qualitative information. One statistical formula may be as effective as twenty pages of text in reporting quantitative information in a manner that is easily understood by those informed in the statistical process.

As presented in this document and in the course of study, statistics is an advanced form of communication, a specialized form of communication using numbers, letters, and symbols as media. Although the word statistics may refer to numerical data, it will be used more generally in the course of study to refer to the body of principles and procedures developed for the collection, classification, and summarization of data. A descriptive statistic is an index number that summarizes or describes a set of data....Inferential statistics is a method that takes chance factors into account when samples are used to reach conclusions about populations. (Spatz, 1997)

Statistics is a substantial component of research language in all the behavioral sciences. Statistics is involved in the research effort from the beginning to end. At the outset statistical terms play a large part in the definition of problems for research. Specific plans for an investigation are formulated to permit statistical evaluations. Data from the investigation are analyzed by statistical methods. Finally, reports of findings are often expressed in statistical terms. Because of accuracy, versatility, and effectiveness in communication, statistics figures prominently in the language, in which researchers theorize, plan, evaluate, speak, and write. Data is a collection of observed values representing one or more characteristics of objects or units. Most social data are in the form of categorical frequencies, cases in defined classes or categories.

Language and Graduate Studies

Early in the development of the university, most academic material was written in Latin and later in German and French. Graduate education, especially at the doctoral level, required a working knowledge of these foreign languages. Since major academic works were in languages other than English, language study was required. Because of advances in the translation of primary data and because the academic center of the world shifted to the United States following World War II, the study of other languages in graduate schools was minimized and statistics was added to the research process.

In days past, just as one would need to know a foreign language to gather primary data, statistics has become a useful tool in gathering and presenting primary data.

In graduate education, participants encounter statistical information in reading previous research. Further, participants present and interpret their research using statistics in order to understand the findings and to clearly communicate the findings. The use of statistics to report research is not as much a mathematical use as a language use, not calculations, but communications. The course of study is not intended to make participants expert statisticians; rather the study is intended to make participants communicators of statistics, both as receivers and senders.

The language of statistics is a part of the culture of academia. In the academic culture, statistics is the primary means of communicating research data. As any language, the language of statistics has grown and evolved. Early English has evolved dynamically into present-day English. In the same way, early statistical language changes dynamically. While the symbols of the language remained the same, the language has progressed from manual mathematics to computer assisted analysis.

The dynamic of change in statistics is similar to the changes in the culture of the automobile. At one time mechanical knowledge of the car was necessary in order to own and drive a car. The dynamic change in ownership of automobiles has changed all of that. The typical driver of today does not need to know details of the mechanics of automobiles in order to drive. All a driver needs to know is where to put in the gas and how to manipulate the controls.

A pilot in ground school learning to fly is taught to compute fuel usage, navigation, weight and balance data, and airspeed by means of a circular slide rule. When the student pilot steps into an airplane, a computer performs most data management.

Statistics has the same dichotomy between what is taught in the classroom and what is expected in actual use of statistics in a research project. Knowing how to compute a standard deviation or Chi square did not help when a researcher was confronted with a totally different problem such as converting questionnaire responses into data for computer analysis. A researcher may have a brilliantly designed project that was approved by a committee and be without sufficient logistical knowledge to bridge from questionnaire to statistical analysis and presentation. The bridge from design to analysis is missing in research literature. The resulting gap has frustrated would-be students of statistics for generations. That gap is perceived as a lack of understanding of the mathematics of statistics but is really a gap in the language of statistics. Math is no longer a major issue. Just as an experienced pilot throws away the circular slide rule, the statistician lays aside the calculator, pen, and pencil and uses the computer.

The computer does the math; the researcher needs primarily to know the language of statistics. The language of statistics is not difficult. The language of statistics can be broken down into three basic components: type of data, number of groups studied, number of measurements. When the data, groups, and measurements are known, the resulting statistical analysis is largely pre-determined, and the computer can easily work the statistical math. To make this work, one must understand the language of data, groups, and measurements.

Behavior as a Statistic

Behavior can be expressed in statistical values, such as sums, means, proportions, differences, or ratios. The student of behavioral science must think about the behavior of people and animals in terms of statistical values. Understanding of behavior as a statistic must develop, not around isolated acts of an individual, but rather around the mean as an evaluation of a number of acts from an individual or a group, or around the proportion of acts that are observed to be in a certain category, or around the differences among individuals and the differences between groups.

Functions of Statistics

Statistical methods in the behavioral sciences serve four related functions. The functions of summarizing, describing, generalizing and experimenting describe the acquisition and communication of new knowledge through research.

Summarizing

The first function of statistics is to summarize research data for communication. A researcher can communicate a mass of information best by condensing and summarizing the information.   A summary is a condensation in which major points of the original account are retained and from which minor points are excluded. The loss of detailed information is regrettable but necessary if the main features of a large amount of data are communicated.

Summarization may involve arranging a set of numbers into a grouped frequency distribution table as an initial step in developing a graph.

Central tendencies can then be easily visualized. Summary statistics is a tool for collecting, condensing, and organizing numerical data.

Describing

The second function of statistics is to describe. Statistical descriptions include measures of central tendency, variability, correlation and regression, the normal distribution, standard scores and graphing methods. Statistics in a text or table communicates with clarity the description of a set of numbers

Generalizing

The third function of statistics is to generalize beyond the limits of a specific investigation to situations that have not been observed. Achieving the first two functions of summarizing and describing is a somewhat limited goal but one that is essential to the meaningfulness of the third function. If what has been observed cannot be expressed clearly and adequately, attributing to the unobserved certainly cannot be done with clarity and meaningfulness.

Results that remain particular usually garner little interest. Particular results that can be generalized, or more accurately can be interpreted, generally garner a great deal of interest. Arguing from the particular to the general is inductive inference. In the long history of arriving at generalized findings, the best solution available has been statistical inference.

Inferential statistics is a valuable body of theory and procedure for generalizing from particular data. Although inference from the particular to the general is subject to error, statistical inference is the best and closest to error-free procedure available. A statistical inference is essentially the act of making and communicating a decision about research results.

Definition: Inferential Statistics goes beyond description to draw conclusions or make predictions by interpreting the data. The two classes of inferential procedures are estimation and hypothesis testing. Frequently used inferential statistics are t statistics, F ratio, and chi-square.

Experimenting

The fourth function was to experiment. Experimental design involves the manipulation of an independent variable in a study to determine the effect on a dependent variable, which is the variable of interest. The group to which the independent variable is assigned is known as the experimental group; the group in which no manipulation occurs is known as the control group. Testing for differences between the experimental group and the control group allows conclusions to be drawn about the effectiveness of the experimental intervention. By contrast, survey research is retrospective. The effects of the independent variables on dependent variables are recorded after they have occurred. The report describes the period of the snap shot.

Counting

Counting is checking the separate units of a collection to determine the total number. The number of observations in a category is known as the frequency. A frequency distribution is a tabular display showing how many individuals possess each value of a particular variable.

Percentages are used to compare groups of unequal size on an equitable basis. The common base for percentage is 100. Regardless of the number being compared in two or more categories, the base of comparison is 100 or more accurately 100% is the whole for each category.

Proportions have a base or total of 1.0. Proportions are always parts of something and can never exceed the total, which is 1.0. Proportions are frequently exchanged for probabilities.

Ratios describe rates and relationships and are fractions. The base, as with a proportion, is 1.0. While proportions are restricted to the relationship of a part to the total, ratios may be used as index numbers. For example, IQ is an index number of the rate of general mental growth to chronological age.

Measurements

Numbers can be used in at least three different ways, depending on the level of measurement. When numbers are used in any fashion, data is created. Numbers may have identity, rank, and additivity. Series of numbers can be used (1) to categorize at the nominal level of measurement, (2) to rank or order at the ordinal level of measurement, and (3) to score at the interval measurement level. Measurement is the assignment of numbers to observations.

Nominal Scale

The nominal scale of measurement is the most limited type of measurement and involves the process of naming or labeling. Nominal measurement can be described as classifying observations into categories. All observations placed in the same category are treated as equal. This is known as the property of identity. The categories must be mutually exclusive, that is, each observation is placed in one and only one category.

The categories must also be exhaustive; that is, a place must be provided for each observation. Nominal data cannot be graded, ranked, or scaled for qualities such as better or worse, higher or lower, more or less. Observations in each category can be counted, which provides a frequency. Demographic data such as groups of ages, gender, nationality, or denominational affiliation are nominal scale data.

There are statistical methods designed to analyze nominal or categorical data. Chi-Square is a primary method of analyzing nominal data.

Ordinal Scale

The ordinal scale of measurement is used when observations can be placed in order, based upon a characteristic. While an order can be observed, the exact measurement between two observations cannot be determined. Thus, the distance between A and B may be much greater than the distance between B and C. The ordinal scale allows for more or less of a characteristic but not how much more or less. An ordinal scale does not have an exact zero nor equal units of measurement. Likert scale items can produce ordinal scale data when the responses are ranked, for example, from one to ten and labels such as 'Agree' and 'Disagree' are attached to each end of the scale. The distance between a response of 3 is only considered to be greater than a response of 2 and smaller than a response of 4. The response of 3 is not considered to be equidistant from 2 and 4.

Because the categories of observations have rank, additional statistical methods of analysis are available including correlation and tests for significant difference. In the survey research example given above a Likert scale item might ask the respondent to circle a number from 1 to 10 with 1 indicating little or no relief from the hiccups and 10 indicating total relief. The researcher could then analyze the differences in the responses among various demographic groups.

Interval Scale

The interval measurement scale involves the application of a scale with equal units and an arbitrary zero. With equal units of measurement, most of the useful numerical operations, such as addition, subtraction, multiplication and division, can be performed. Temperature readings on a Celsius or Fahrenheit thermometer and individual intelligence test scores like the Stanford-Binet or the Wechsler tests are examples of interval data. The measurement of zero on interval scales does not mean the absence of the trait being measured, simply that the scale was not sensitive enough to measure levels of the variable below a certain point. Interval data analysis involves the use of powerful statistical methods such as correlation, t-Tests, and Analysis of Variance (ANOVA).

Ratio Scale

A ratio measurement scale is very much like an interval measurement scale except the observations have an absolute zero. Dollars or cents, yards or feet, minutes or seconds and cash on hand are all ratio measurements or measurements on a ratio scale. Practically speaking, ratio data are equivalent to interval data and may be analyzed by many of the same statistical methods.

Hypothesis Testing

In the behavioral sciences, research is conducted to determine the acceptability of hypotheses derived from theories of behavior. The researcher develops a hypothesis from a theory and collects empirical data to determine the acceptability of the hypothesis. The empirical data may lead to retaining, revising or rejecting the hypothesis and/or the theory from which the hypothesis was developed. (Siegel 1956).

A research hypothesis is a statement of theory, previous

research results, or other information that leads to an anticipated outcome. The null hypothesis is a hypothesis of no differences. According to the null hypothesis, any observed difference between samples is regarded as a chance occurrence resulting from sampling error alone. If the null hypothesis of no difference is rejected, the alternate hypothesis that a true population or sample difference does exist is accepted. An alternative hypothesis is a claim about a population parameter that will be true if the null hypothesis is false.

In order to make an objective decision about whether a particular hypothesis is confirmed by a set of data, objective procedures are needed. Following are a set of procedures in order of performance that can be used to determine the disposition of a null hypothesis: (1) state the null hypothesis (Ho), (2) choose a statistical test for testing Ho, (3) specify a significance level (a) and a sample size (n), (4) find / assume the sampling distribution of the statistical test under Ho, (5) define the region of rejection, and (6) compute the value of the statistical test, using the data obtained from the sample(s). If the computed value is in the region of rejection, reject Ho. If the computed value is outside the region of rejection, Ho cannot be rejected at the chosen level of significance.

Significance level of a test is the probability of rejecting Ho when in fact it is true. The size of the rejection region depends on the value assigned to α. The commonly used values of α are 0.01, 0.05, and 0.10. In social science research, the most common value of α is 0.05. The critical value or critical point is the place on a curve at which the rejection and non-rejection regions are divided.

Objective Decision
A few questions about a set of data can lead quickly to a

decision about which statistical procedure is most appropriate.

1) What type of measurement scale produced the data – nominal, ordinal, or interval/ratio scale?

2) Was the data related or independent? Was there an absence of association between observations or were the observations related as in a pre-test/post-test of the same group?

3) Was the group(s) randomly selected?

4) Was the data normally distributed?

5) How many groups and how many measurements are involved?

All Data contains Error

A basic assumption of statistics is that all data contains error; therefore, a major task of written material is to guard against false statements, weak reasoning, or a poor choice of words. Since the meaning of words is in the reader, one must use words that are clearly understood and free from equivocation, or using the same word in two different senses in the material; such as a lot for sale and a lot of stuff.

The best way to study statistics is to see statistics as a language rather than a mathematical process. The English language is a difficult one; it is ambiguous and borrows many words and concepts from other languages and cultures. Better understanding the English language and seeing statistics as a language and a communication system, the process of education is greatly simplified.

Topics Discussed in Chapter Eight

A Rationalist View
The Empiricist Approach

ASSUMPTIONS ABOUT LANGUAGE

Fallacy of Equivocation

The first assumption about language is the belief that all language is incapable of expressing literal truth. An interesting fallacy is committed by many proponents of this position. First, these proponents point to the undeniable fact that all language is symbolic. From this fact, they infer that no language can be literally true. The specific error here goes by the name of the fallacy of equivocation, an error committed whenever a key word in an argument is used in two different senses.

The word *symbolic* can mean either: (1) non-literal or (2) that which serves as a symbol or representation for something else. It is undeniably (literally?) true that all language is symbolic in the second sense. But, if the word *symbol* is used in the argument in question in this second sense, the conclusion does not follow. If "symbol" is used in the first sense, the conclusion does follow but the argument is trivial. That is, it simply states: all language is non-literal; therefore, no language can be literal.

Language can serve a variety of functions. Many times, it is meant to be taken metaphorically or non-literally. But the possibility of non-literal uses of language requires that there are also uses of language in which it is meant to be taken literally. If no language is capable of expressing literal truth, then, of course, it follows that even God cannot use language to communicate literal truth. But those who appeal to this argument conveniently ignore some of the fallout from their position. For example, if no language can be literally true, then it is also impossible for philosophers and theologians (including those who hold this position) to convey their thoughts in literally true propositions. Ironically, many of these writers act as if their sentences do convey literal truth.

The second alien presupposition is the claim that human language is derived from sensible human experience of the visible world. If this were true, it would be difficult to see how such a language could be adequate to express truth about a spiritual world and a transcendent being. Even if St. Paul, for example, had in some way received an intelligible revelation, how could he have communicated it to others? But before we get too excited about the supposed problem, we should look more carefully at the theory that gives rise to it.

Empiricism

Theories of knowledge may be either empiricist or rationalist. It is empiricism that gives rise to views of language that cannot account for the possibility of communication about non-sensible reality. How might the differences between rationalism and empiricism as theories of knowledge give rise to competing theories of language? One way to see this is to return to the model of the mind as a blank tablet. If the empiricist is correct and the human mind at birth is like a blank tablet, then in principle every feature of human language should be explicable in terms of what human beings acquire through their experiences of the world.

Language and Thought

The linguist Chomsky has received much attention for rejecting the empiricist and behaviorist accounts of the origin of language. His own view stresses the relationship between language and thought. Language, in his view, does not grow out of human experience. Instead, he maintains, language is made possible by human thought. "As far as we know," Chomsky wrote, "human language is associated with a specific type of mental organization, not simply a higher degree of intelligence." (Chomsky, 1968)

The actual use of language is far more complex than the accumulated total of input experience. Children learn the use of grammar very early in their lives. But their mastery of a grammar goes far beyond the sum total of things they have heard or learned. Children are soon able to speak and write new sentences unlike any they have heard or read. Thus, the actual use of language contains many characteristics that cannot be accounted for on the basis of stimulus and response.

When a human being uses language, far more is put out than sense experience ever put in. Human beings use grammar creatively. We are able to use and comprehend sentences unlike any heard or used in previous experience. In fact, most of the sentences we use and understand are new ones never encountered in prior experience. Chomsky believes this feature of language is explained by our possession of unconscious, innate knowledge of the rules of language. Returning to the box model, if output regularly exceeds input, the box must have contributed something. Chomsky concludes that the mind must contribute something to language learning. Because any particular grammar is able to generate an infinite number of new and different sentences, it must follow that knowledge of a language is the complex result of an interaction of input from one's environment and an innate structure of the human mind. (Cromsky, 1965)

Chomsky represents a rationalist approach to the theory of language; he stresses the primacy of mind and thought with respect to language building. The fundamental similarity of all human languages, Chomsky believes, suggests that the human brain contains an innate disposition to build grammar. Human beings come into the world already equipped with an innate ability to acquire and use language and to construct grammar. The principles of language are not acquired; they are present innately in every normal human mind at birth. Children utilize this innate knowledge when they learn the grammar of their own language. Language does not grow out of human experience. Instead, Chomsky maintains, language is made possible by human thought.

The Empiricist Approach

Basic to the empiricist approach to language is the belief that language like human knowledge arises from sense experience; language grows out of children's imitation of their parents' use of language. Since, on this view, words have their origin in sense experience, the original referent for any word must be something physical. Even words that denote relations are supposed to arise from an experience of spatial relations. Not surprisingly, advocates of such a theory of language conclude that human language cannot apply literally to things that are spiritual and non-spatial.

All theologians use words like *soul* and *God* to refer to things that are spiritual and non-spatial. How can words that supposedly have an original physical referent suddenly refer adequately to something spiritual? Is it possible that some theologians have been too hasty in accepting an empiricist theory of language? "If all words are primarily physical or sensuous, and if relations are basically spatial, either language cannot properly apply to spiritual and non-spatial subjects, or one must explain how the physical meaning can be changed into a spiritual meaning. How can sensory experience give rise to words for soul and God?" (Clark, 1991)

Carl Henry extened his critique:

> The prevalent contemporary theory that language originates in sense experience and represents a gradual evolutionary development of animal sounds is difficult to assess because its supposed stages have not been exhibited, and because there are striking differences between nonhuman utterances. Contrary to human language that communicates a descriptive content and changes from time to time and place to place, the sounds of birds and beasts are instinctive and constant, and can hardly be considered descriptive sentences. If words are primarily sensuous in their reference, as naturalism contends, and are not to be considered signs of a mental concept, nor to be correlated with intellection, then it should be emphasized that such explanation is not verified by the empirical criteria that naturalism cherishes. (Henry, 1976-1983)

Karl Barth is an example of those theologians who regard human language as an unfit instrument to carry the truth of God. When one thinks of God, according to Barth, the words used are unworthy of God and are inappropriate to express a clear knowledge of God. This suspicion that words are generally unfit to carry anything as majestic as God's revelation is one element of the contemporary rejection of prepositional revelation. Words themselves should never be regarded as God's revelation. At most, they can witness to the revelation; God may use words to "communicate" with human beings. But once again, the appearance of such views in a theologian who himself has written hundreds of thousands of words about God is more than a little ironic. Barth has told us that human language cannot be used to speak truly about God; God is simply too great for human language. What are we to make then of the thousands of sentences that Barth has written about God?

James Packer has drawn attention to several claims used by theologians like Barth to ground their skepticism about human language. (1) They assert that language is an inadequate instrument of human communication. But their view is obviously self-defeating. Consider the dilemma it raises for the person who holds this view. Either his own use of language is an exception to his claim or it is not. If his own language is an exception, then some uses of language can be an adequate instrument of human communication, in which case claim (1) is false. But if the proponent's own language is not an exception to his theory, his view can be safely ignored since on his own view he cannot possibly communicate that theory to us.

A second claim Packer identifies is that made by the theological skeptic who thinks that no human language can communicate information about transcendent reality. Few of the theologians who assert claim (2) practice what they preach. Any theologian who asserts (a) that human language cannot communicate information about the transcendent and (b) that God is transcendent is, of course, caught in a contradiction. The statement that God is transcendent is a communication about transcendent reality. Any advocate of claim (2) who wishes to be consistent must become dumb and forfeit forever the right to say anything about God. This is an interesting prospect to contemplate.

The third position that Packer finds in the thinking of those skeptical about religious language is the denial that the language of Scripture is a prepositional revelation of divine truth. Since we have already devoted two chapters to this unfortunate position, no further comment is needed except to note, with Packer, that the disjunction between personal and prepositional revelation "makes God's method of self-disclosure analogous to the nonverbal communication of Harpo Marx." (Packer, 1980)

When leaders of theology thus decline to treat any of the statements of our thousand-plus-page, million-and-a-half word Bible as information from God to us and trumpet abroad that these can be no such thing as God-given information and that it is an intellectual mistake to look for any, it is no wonder if folk lose faith in the capacity of biblical speech to tell us facts about our Maker. Were we all clearheadedly logical, we should see ourselves as called by this situation to choose between such modern theologians . . . and such older ones as Moses and the prophets, Jesus Christ, Peter, Paul, John, and the author of Hebrews. Seeing the issue that way we might resolve that, on this point at least, we should ditch the moderns.

What reasons are given to support the three claims just noted? Considering their significance, it is surprising to find hardly any. Modern theologians seem to regard these claims as self-evident, so that no support is really needed. That confidence is unwarranted. The truth seems to be that no support can be given.

What theory of language do I offer in lieu of the basically

empiricist position that grounds the prevailing skepticism toward language as a vehicle of divine revelation? My alternative view flows naturally from my acceptance of a Logos epistemology: The omnipotent God has created human beings as rational creatures who possess innately the capacity to think and to use language. Language is possible because humans, created in the image of God, possess innately a priori categories of thought and the ability to use and understand language.

As Carl Henry explained:

> Since every mind is lighted by the Logos or Reason of God, thought stands behind language . . . Man's ability to think and to speak (is) God-given for certain essential purposes—for receiving a verbal revelation, for approaching God in prayer, and for conversing with others about God and spiritual realities . . . The gift of human speech and language, in brief, presupposes the *imago Dei,* particularly rationality. (Henry, 1976-1983)

Thought exists behind language as its necessary condition. Communication is possible because the human creatures using language are enlightened by the divine Logos, are in possession of certain innate ideas. Humans can communicate only when they share the same ideas. "The situation," Gordon Clark says, "is somewhat like that of cryptographers who can break any cipher. The symbols are at first unknown; but because the ideas expressed are common, the message can be understood. If language had no thought behind it, as the behaviorists claim, and if the symbols were just a random aggregate of marks, there would be no cipher to break." Therefore, the sufficiency of human language to communicate truth about a transcendent God rests on "the theomorphism of created man, whom God made a language user, able to receive

God's linguistic communication and to respond in kind."

Basic to the Christian worldview is the presupposition that the human being is a creature who carries the image of God. Essential to this image is rationality, a rationality that reflects the rationality of God's own mind. Human language is adequate as a vehicle for divine revelation and for human communication about God because it is a divinely given instrument. God can; therefore, reveal truth about Himself through words.

Bibliography

Apps, Jerold W. (1992), <u>Study Skills for Adults Returning to School</u>. New York: McGraw-Hill Book Company.

Augustine: <u>Teaching Christianity [De Doctrina Christiana]</u>. Translated by Edmund Hill, in <u>The Works of Saint Augustine: A Translation for the 21st Century</u>. Part I, Vol. 11, edited by John E, Rotelle. Hyde Park, New York: New City Press, 1996.

Bernstein, Richard J. (1983), <u>Beyond Objectivism and Relativism: Science, Hermeneutics, and Praxis</u>. Philadelphia: University of Pennsylvania Press.

Bray, Gerald, (1996), <u>Biblical Interpretation Past and Present</u>. Downers Grove, Illinois: InterVarsity Press.

Bruns, Gerald L. (1992) <u>Hermeneutics Ancient and Modern</u>. Yale Studies in Hermeneutics. New Haven and London: Yale University Press.

Calkins, Lucy McCormick. (1994), <u>The Art of Teaching Writing</u>, New Edition. Portsmouth, N.H.: Heinemann.

Carney, Tom, and Barbara Carney. (1998), <u>Liberation Learning: Self-Directed Learning for Students</u>. Windsor, Ontario: Para-Publishing Enterprises.

Carson, Donald A.,(1984), <u>Exegetical Fallacies</u>. Grand Rapids: Baker Book House.

Chomsky, Noam (1968) <u>Language and Mind</u>, New York: Harper & Row.

Chomsky, Noam, (1965) <u>Aspects of the Theory of Syntax</u>, Cambridge: MIT Press.

Clark, Gordon H.(1991), Religion, Reason and Revelation,
        Jefferson: Trinity Foundation.
Corley Bruce, Steve Lemke, and Grant Lovejoy, eds.
        Biblical Hermeneutics: A Comprehensive
Introduction to Interpreting Scripture. Nashville:
        Broadman and Holman, 1996. 2nd ed. 2002.
Dyck, Elmer, (editor),(1996) The Act of Bible Reading:
        A Multidisciplinary Approach to Biblical Interpreta
        tion. Downers Grove, Illinois: InterVarsity Press.
Ewen, R.B. (1988), The Workbook for Introductory
        Statistics for the Behavioral Sciences. Orlando, FL:
        Harcourt Brace Jovanovich.
Fee, Gordon D. , (1993) New Testament Exegesis:
        A Handbook for Students and Pastors. Louisville,
        Kentucky: Westminster/John Knox Press.
Geisler, Norman L., (1983), Explaining Hermeneutics:
        A Commentary on the Chicago Statement on Biblical
        Hermeneutics. Oakland, California:
        International Council on Biblical Inerrancy.
Grondin, Jean. (1994), Introduction to Philosophical
        Hermeneutics. Translated by Joel Weinsheimer.
        New Haven: Yale University Press.
Henry, Carl R. H., (1976-1983), God, Revelation and
        Authority, Volume I-VI, Waco, TX: Word Books,
Hirsch Jr., E.D. (1967), Validity in Interpretation. New
        Haven: Yale University Press.
Jackson, Norma R. with Paul L. Pillow, (1992), The Reading
        -Writing Workshop: Getting Started. New York:
        Scholastic.

Johns, J.L., VanLeirsburg, P., & Davis, S.J., (1994), Improving Reading: A Handbook of Strategies. Dubuque, IA: Kendall/Hunt Publishing Co.

Johnson, Elliott E., (1990), Expository Hermeneutics: An Introduction. Grand Rapids: Zondervan.

Julian, Ron, David Crabtree and Jack Crabtree, (2001), The Language of God: A Common Sense Approach to Understanding and Applying the Bible. Colorado Springs: NavPress.

Kolstoe, R.H. (1969). Introduction to Statistics for the Behavioral Sciences. Homewood, ILL: Dorsey.

Levin, J., and James, A.F. (1991). Elementary Statistics in Social Research, 5th ed. New York: HarperCollins.

Long, V. Philips, Tremper Longman III, Moises Silva, and Vern Sheridan Poythress. Foundations of Contemporary Interpretation. Six volumes in one. Grand Rapids: Zondervan, 1996.

Packer, James I., (1980), The Adequacy of Human Language in Inerrancy, Ed. Norman L. Geisler, Grand Rapids: Zondervan.

Sall, Creighton & Lehman, JMP Start Statistics 3ed, 2005, Thomson Brooks/Cole.

Siegel, (1956), Nonparametric Statistics, McGraw-Hill.

Snedecor & Cochran, Statistical Methods, 8ed, 1989, Iowa State University Press.

Zuck, Roy B. ed. Rightly Divided: Readings in Biblical Hermeneutics. Grand Rapids: Kregel Publishing, 1996.

Other Titles by Hollis L. Green, ThD, PhD

General Books
>
> Designing Valid Research
> Discipleship
> Fighting the Amalekites
> Hitch your Star to a Wagon
> Integrating Moral Values
> Interpreting an Author's Words
> Marching As To War
> Philosophy of Adult Education
> Sympathetic Leadership Cybernetics
> Titanic Lessons
> Understanding Graduate Research
> Understanding Pentecostalism
> Understanding Scientific Research
> Where in the World are you Going?
> Why Christianity Fails in America
> Why Churches Die
> Why Wait Till Sunday?

Coffee Table Books
>
> Love's Extended Conversation
> SO TALES - Vol. I
> - Preachers and the Ministry
> SO TALES Vol. II
> - Childhood, Cousins, and Consequences
> SO TALES Vol. III
> - Domestic and Foreign Travel
> SO TALES Vol. IV
> - Courtship, Marriage, and Relatives
> Things Learned and Passed to my Sons

Children's Books
        SLEEPY TOWN Lullaby and Story
        The Scoop about Birthday Soup
        The Cat that Ate the Birthday Cake
        The Funky Chicken and the Hillbilly Rooster
        The Frog that Couldn't Croak
        Tea Party at Nany Park's House
        The Boy that wanted to Grow a Beard
        Ditala - The Boy that Killed the Dead Snake
        The Boys that couldn't find the Big Dripper.
        The Trouble with Funny Book Cussing
        The Mouse of the House
 Books in Process
        All Believers are Created Equal
        Growing a New Testament Church
        Lessons from Luke – NT 101
        How to Build a Better Spouse Trap
        EVERGREEN Devotional New Testament
        Volume One:
        Relational Epistles
        Volume Two:
        Epistles Addressed to Scattered Believers
        Volume Three:
        Christian Foundation and Church Development
        Volume Four:
        Epistles to Believers in Churches

Check availability and order at website:
        (www.globaledadvance.org)

Interpreting An Author's Words
Refine Study and Writing Skills
By Understanding the Written Word

GlobalEdAdvancePress
37321-7635 USA
GlobalEdAdvance@aol.com

ISBN978-0-9801674-7-4

www.ingramcontent.com/pod-product-compliance
Lightning Source LLC
Chambersburg PA
CBHW060545100426
42742CB00013B/2455